Pasta Salad

Pasta Salad

50 FAVORITE RECIPES

by Barbara Lauterbach

Photographs by Reed Davis

CHRONICLE BOOKS

SAN FRANCISCO

LIBRARY OF CONGRESS CATALOGING-IN-PUBLICATION DATA:
Lauterbach, Barbara.
Pasta salad : 50 favorite recipes / by Barbara Lauterbach;
photographs by Reed Davis.
108p. 22.3 x 20.4cm.
ISBN 0-8118-4203-7 (pbk.)
1. Pasta salads. 2. Cookery (Pasta) I. Title.
TX809.M17 .L38 2004
641.8'22—dc22
2003020324

Manufactured in China.

CHRONICLE BOOKS LLC
85 Second Street
San Francisco, California 94105
www.chroniclebooks.com

FOOD & PROP STYLING BY Rori Trovato
DESIGNED AND TYPESET BY NOON / www.designatnoon.com

Distributed in Canada by Raincoast Books
9050 Shaughnessy Street
Vancouver, British Columbia V6P 6E5

10 9 8 7 6 5 4 3 2 1

PAGE 02: *"Meredith in Bloom" Picnic Pasta Salad with Roasted Asparagus, page 50.*

TO THE WWW'S (WONDERFUL WOMEN WALKING) FOR THEIR LISTENING, TESTING, AND TASTING, BUT ABOVE ALL ELSE, FRIENDSHIP, CINDY BARNES, NANCY CURRAN, PHYLLIS HAMBLET, LINDA HUNTRESS, MY WONDERFUL ASSISTANT LIZ LAPHAM, FRAN SECORD, DENNY STRINGFELLOW, AND MARIAN TOUHEY.

ACKNOWLEDGMENTS

Deepest thanks to my agent Susan Ginsburg for her encouragement and support throughout the process. So many people contributed to this book, thank you all for your generous contributions of time, tasting and testing. Dan Bryant, Lisa and Bill Laskin, "CH" and Lisa Lauterbach, Ellen Ogden, Kathryn Ellis Moore, Ann Alspaugh and Margaret Vallion, Mary Lee and her sons Alex and Andy Bickford, Jo, Tom, Greg and Carlie Duval, Helen Heiner, Maxiene Glenday, Megan Dodge, Patte Morrow, Wendy Van de Poll, Robby Graham, Louis Ellenbogen, Anne McNeill, Don Ziemba. And last but not least, Kimberly Humann of Barilla Pasta.

To the wonderful people at Chronicle, with whom it is a great pleasure to be associated: My editor Bill LeBlond for believing this book could happen, Amy Treadwell, who shared not only her knowledge but friendship, and Holly Burrows.

Cinthia Wen for a beautifully designed book and Reed Davis, who once again has taken a white subject and brought it to life vividly.

Jan Hughes and Doug Ogan again for their careful editing, and Carrie Bradley as copyeditor, Benjamin Shaykin as art director, Michelle Fuller, again as publicist, and Christi Cavallaro for her marketing skills. My deepest thanks and affection to you all, you are an extraordinary team.

:: table of contents

6

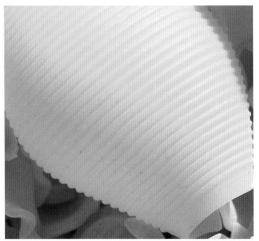
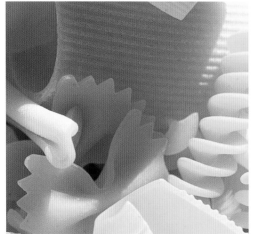
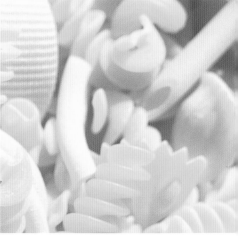
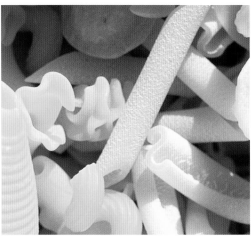

the basics

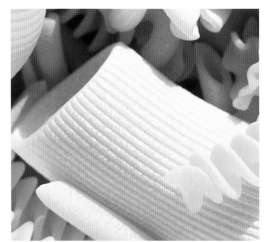
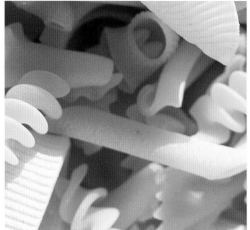

Introduction

When it comes to pasta salad, you need to think outside the elbow. Elbow macaroni, that is. Otherwise you are likely to ignore some wonderful dishes by grouping them with the ubiquitous community potluck/church supper favorite of yesteryear. This old favorite often sacrificed taste and texture for bulk. The ingredients—often overcooked macaroni, celery, onion and a bit of radish or carrot for color—would be bound together with too much mayonnaise or a sweetened salad cream dressing. Many of today's soggy deli creations perpetuate that heritage and the unfair rap it lays on the pasta salad genre. Too long relegated to the bottom of the salad chain, pasta salad deserves a revisit.

America's love affair with pasta beyond macaroni and spaghetti became close to a national obsession as increasingly more Americans traveled abroad. Once back home we took our passion, as is our nature, one step further. In the land of the free and the home of the entrepreneur, we "saladized" it. As a nation, we probably eat more concoctions that are labeled "salad" than any other country do in the world. Although most true Italian cooks have little or no use for American deli pasta salad, a really well made pasta salad has a definite place on the table.

Indeed, a properly prepared pasta salad, lightly dressed and glistening with tubes, twists or bows of cool pasta, embellished with crunchy morsels of vegetables, succulent cubes of chicken or chunks of tender sweet lobster meat, can hold its head up in any culinary company. It can be the star of a summer's eve menu or amenable supporting player at a buffet or picnic.

The difference between a mediocre, dull pasta salad and a delicious one lies in following a few easy ground rules of preparation, which this book will provide.

Which pastas are suitable for salads will be discussed, as well as how to cook the pasta correctly. Information on the correct selection of oils and vinegars for the all-important salad dressing will be included, with a nod to the mayonnaise-based salad, and how to circumvent the pitfalls of a soggy concoction. Tasty sauces and vinaigrettes appropriate for salads will be presented, as well as master recipes for useful techniques such as roasting peppers and toasting nuts.

The good news for today's busy cook is that most of the steps in making a pasta salad can be done ahead. Many of the ingredients are inexpensive and interchangeable. As a cooking teacher of many years, I know my students want to present a dish that does not require last minute preparation but looks and tastes as if they had spent effort in preparing it. The methods and recipes in this book will help you achieve this goal. Together, we'll think outside the elbow!

The Long and the Short of It: The Best Choice of Pasta for Salad

The best choice of pasta for salad is good-quality commercial dry pasta.

These can be divided into three groups by shape: long, short, and small pasta for soup.

Within these combined categories are more than three hundred shapes, many with wonderfully lyrical names. Commercial pasta made with durum wheat semolina is the most suitable for cold dishes, as it produces a firmer cooked product due to the high gluten content of the flour. Commercial pasta can be made with common wheat flour, but it does not hold up well for a cold preparation, as it tends to be stickier when cooked. The label on the package tells what flour was used for the pasta inside.

Short pasta shapes are the most suitable for trapping dressing and bits of ingredients, thereby producing rich bursts of flavor; for that reason, the longer shapes are less commonly used for pasta salads. Long Asian rice noodles, however, are a popular foundation for salads. The short pasta shapes are, for the most part, interchangeable in the recipes that follow. The small soup pastas are rarely used in salads, with the exception of the ricelike orzo.

Homemade pasta, while delicious when swathed in a warm sauce, does not adapt itself to a cold salad preparation.

ASIAN NOODLES

Distinguishing between the types of rice noodles used in many Asian preparations can be confusing at best to the purchaser. Used in the cuisines of China, Malaysia, and Thailand, among others, the thick white noodles resembling ribbon pasta are sometimes called rice noodles, sometimes rice sticks. The thin varieties of rice noodle may also be called rice sticks, or else vermicelli, as they resemble the flour-based vermicelli of Western cuisine. Thin cellophane noodles made from the starch of mung beans are also sold as vermicelli. The bottom line is, buy the shape you want regardless of the name, as the English translations of the names are simply not consistent. Asian markets have fresh rice noodles as well, but like fresh pasta, they do not work well for cold noodle preparations.

Japanese noodles also vary. Soba noodles are made from buckwheat flour and are most often eaten cold, whereas udon noodles are made from whole-wheat flour and generally served in soups. Somen noodles are thinner and are used in both soups and cold dishes.

Be sure to read the ingredients list on the package for any Asian noodle and avoid those that contain cornstarch, which produce a softer, mushier noodle when cooked. It is also best to follow the cooking directions on the package; many manufacturers differentiate methods of preparation depending on whether you're using the noodles for cold salads, stir-fry, or soup. Read the box!

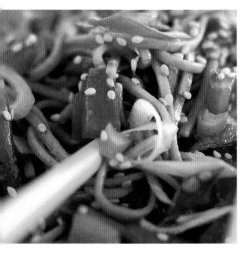

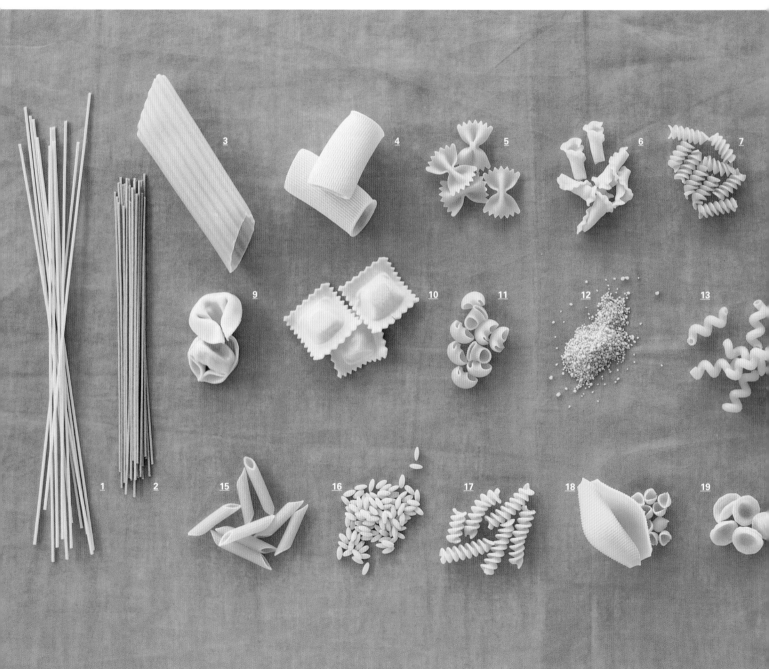

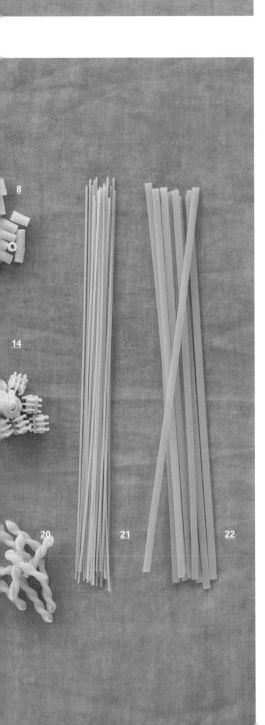

Although I have called for specific pastas in many of the recipes in this book, they are for the most part interchangeable. I have selected pastas readily available in supermarkets. This list of the pastas called for in the book gives you a brief description of their shape and appearance.

01	UDON	Thin, yellow strands
02	SOBA	Thin, brown strands
03	MANICOTTI	Large tubes for stuffing, about 4 inches long
04	RIGATONI	Large, ridged tubes, about 1½ inches long
05	FARFALLE	Bow-tie shapes (*"butterflies"*)
06	CAMPANELLE	Bell shapes (*"little bells"*)
07	ROTINI	Short spirals, also available in tricolor (*white, red, and green*)
08	DITALINI	Very short tubes
09	TORTELLINI	Small ring-shaped pasta stuffed with meat or vegetables
10	RAVIOLI	Bite-sized round or square stuffed pasta
11	PIPETTE	Small, ridged, elbow shapes (*"little pipes"*)
12	COUSCOUS	Granular semolina
13	CELLENTANI	Short, twisted, ridged tubes
14	RADIATORE	Short, twisted shapes with deep ridges (*"little radiators"*)
15	PENNE	Smooth or ridged tubes cut diagonally (*"pens" or "quills"*)
16	ORZO	Small rice-shaped pasta (*"barley"*)
17	FUSILLI	Spiral, both short and long (*"little springs"*)
18	CONCHIGLIE	Small, medium, and large ridged, shell shapes
19	ORECCHIETTE	Small, round, flat pillows (*"little ears"*)
20	GEMELLI	Two short strands twisted together (*"twins"*)
21	VERMICELLI	Very thin, long strands (*"little worms"*)
22	FETTUCCINE	flat ribbon pasta, about ¼ inch wide (*"little ribbons"*)
	RICE NOODLES	White ribbon noodle (*not pictured*)

How to Cook Pasta for Salad

One of the most important things in making pasta salad is cooking the pasta correctly. If pasta salad sometimes gets a bad name, it is often because the cook has not followed a few simple ground rules. These are:

- Use a large pot. It does not have to be an expensive stainless steel pot; actually, water will come to a boil more rapidly in a thinner, less expensive pot. Use an 8-quart pot and 4 quarts of water for 1 pound of pasta.

- Bring the water to a rolling boil. Add the salt (see the table below) and stir to dissolve. Salt adds flavor and helps ensure firmness. Add the pasta all at once, raise the heat, and stir briefly with a wooden spoon. If the boil subsides too much, cover the pot with a lid for a very short time until the water returns to the boil. Remove the lid to continue cooking.

- Cook the pasta for the time recommended on the box. For salad, this should be *al dente,* or "to the tooth," that is, cooked throughout, but still firm to the bite. If the pasta you purchase does not have instructions for *al dente* on the package, cook it for the minimum time suggested. Taste the pasta a minute before it is due to be done to guard against overcooking. When it is *al dente,* drain the pasta into a colander and rinse briefly under cold running water. (You do not need to rinse for hot pasta dishes, as the starch helps the sauce cling to the pasta.)

- When cooking Asian noodles, after placing the noodles in the boiling water, stir them occasionally with a long-pronged fork in the first few minutes of cooking, as they tend to clump together.

- If cooking the pasta ahead of time, drizzle a little oil over the drained pasta, toss to coat, cover, and refrigerate until ready to proceed with the recipe.

- Many pasta salads benefit from a resting time, as the pasta absorbs the dressing, resulting in a fuller flavor. If left too long however, they will tend to dry out.

PROPORTIONS IN THE POT

Here is a guide to the amount of water and salt to use with the given amount of pasta.

PASTA	WATER	SALT
6 ounces	3 quarts	1½ teaspoons
8 to 12 ounces	4 quarts	2 teaspoons
1 pound	5 quarts	1 tablespoon

Pasta expands in size as it cooks, so it is useful to know how much the dry quantity will yield. Here is a guide to various shapes and their yields.

SHAPE	DRY	COOKED
Conchiglie, orecchiette, and similar shapes	8 ounces	4 cups
Farfalle and similar shapes	8 ounces	5 cups
Fettuccini and similar ribbons	8 ounces	3¼ cups
Orzo	8 ounces	3 cups
Rotini, penne, and similar shapes	8 ounces	4 cups
Vermicelli	8 ounces	4½ cups

Salad Smarts

- If you are preparing your greens or fresh herbs for salad several hours ahead of time, wrap them in dampened paper towels and store them in sealable bags in the refrigerator.

- When chopping on a small board, place a dampened kitchen towel under the board to keep it steady.

- To seed a tomato, cut the tomato in half horizontally. Take one tomato half in your hand, squeeze it gently, and then flick your wrist with the tomato sharply several times over a sink (or a bowl if you need the pulp). The seeds will fall right out.

- To cut basil into chiffonade, stack six to eight leaves on top of each other, roll them up in a tube, and cut thinly crosswise across the tube. Repeat until you have used all the leaves. This is more satisfactory than chopping basil for many salads; you will have lovely shreds of basil.

- If a salad recipe calls for red onion, marinate the sliced onion in fresh lime juice for 1 hour. The onion will develop a sweet-and-sour flavor that adds another dimension to the finished dish.

- To remove the pits from olives, place several olives at a time on a cutting board and position the flat side of a chef's knife over them. Hit the blade of the knife with the palm of your hand. The olives should split open and the pits will pop out.

- When mixing dressing in a bowl, place a dampened kitchen towel under the bowl before whisking. This will keep the bowl from traveling while you whisk.

- When measuring honey, spray the measuring cup or spoon with vegetable-oil spray first; the honey will slide right off.

- Two plastic spatulas work well for tossing pasta salad, as they do not break up the ingredients as metal spoons or forks can.

- Many salads benefit from being served on a large platter instead of the traditional deep salad bowl. When served in this manner, all the "goodies" do not sink to the bottom of the bowl.

CHAPTER 2 : master recipes

Vinaigrette

A pasta salad—or any salad—can rise or fall on the dressing; therefore, a classic vinaigrette should be in every self-respecting cook's repertoire. A mixture of acidic liquid and oil, vinaigrette can easily be adapted to suit the salad at hand. The general rule of thumb is one part acidic liquid, such as vinegar or lemon juice, to three or four parts oil. Certain vinegars and citrus juices are less acidic and oil flavors vary immensely, so it's best to customize your vinaigrette to the salad you are making. A lot depends on your personal preference: Do you like a sharp and tangy dressing, or do you prefer a mellower taste?

The most popular oil for a vinaigrette dressing is extra-virgin olive oil, the oil from the first pressing of the olives. Other popular oil choices are grapeseed, canola, peanut, corn, and safflower. The most common accent oils (those too strongly flavored to be used alone but which work well in combination with a more neutral oil) are walnut and Asian sesame oils.

Red and white wine vinegar are the most frequently used acidic choices, with the fresh taste of lemon juice being popular as well. The rich flavor of balsamic vinegar works in some dressings, as does rice wine vinegar, a mild, less-acidic vinegar used primarily in Asian vinaigrettes.

The two liquids in a vinaigrette are coaxed into an emulsion, which means that they are incorporated together by whisking vigorously, making a creamy dressing. If whisked by hand, the mixture will break down quickly, so you will need to whisk it again before pouring it over a salad. If you use a food processor or blender, the emulsion will last much longer. You may also shake all the ingredients in a jar.

Salt and pepper are added to the acidic liquid before mixing with the oil. Adding the salt at this point allows it to "melt" into the dressing. A little Dijon mustard can be added to the vinegar or citrus juice; it aids in the emulsification process and sharpens the flavor. There are many other optional ingredients to customize your dressing; you can also add anchovy paste, shallots, minced garlic, or even a pinch of sugar if the dressing is too sharp for your taste. Fresh herbs are generally added after the oil for maximum flavor.

BASIC VINAIGRETTE

MAKES ½ CUP

- 2 tablespoons good-quality red or white wine vinegar
- Salt and freshly ground black pepper
- ¼ teaspoon Dijon mustard *(optional)*
- 1 teaspoon minced garlic or shallot *(optional)*
- ⅓ cup extra-virgin olive oil

PREPARATION

In a small bowl, combine the vinegar and, starting with ¼ teaspoon each, the salt and pepper to taste. Add the mustard and garlic or shallot, if using. Slowly, drop by drop, whisk in the olive oil, whisking constantly until the two liquids have combined smoothly into an emulsion.

The vinaigrette is best used fresh but may be stored, covered and refrigerated, for 1 day.

Mayonnaise

Homemade mayonnaise is not difficult to master, and it is a skill worth knowing, as the fresh flavor of homemade mayonnaise is delicious. However, some cooks prefer not to use raw eggs. The presence of salmonella bacteria is possible, although contamination is very rare. If you are concerned, any good-quality commercial mayonnaise can be used in place of homemade in the recipes in this book. In my experience, mayonnaise recipes calling for partially cooked eggs are neither very good nor worth the trouble.

Deciding which type of oil to use in the mayonnaise demands a good look at the salad to be dressed. The appropriate degree of robustness of the oil depends on the ingredients in the salad. A salad composed of strong flavors can take a dressing made with a large proportion of heavier oil, such as a full-bodied olive oil. For a salad with subtler flavors, consider mixing 1 cup vegetable oil and ½ cup olive oil, or a combination of vegetable and peanut or even walnut oils.

BASIC MAYONNAISE

MAKES I CUP

○ 1 large whole egg, plus 1 large egg yolk
○ 1½ teaspoons prepared Dijon mustard
○ 1 tablespoon fresh lemon juice or white wine vinegar
○ Salt and freshly ground black pepper
○ 1½ cups vegetable oil

PREPARATION

To make in a food processor or blender: Combine the whole egg, egg yolk, mustard, lemon juice, and salt and pepper to taste in the food processor or blender. Process for 20 seconds to "melt" the salt and thicken the egg. With the motor running, add the oil as slowly as you can at first, just a dribble, increasing the flow as you see the mixture thickening and becoming creamy. When all of the oil has been added, taste and adjust the seasoning. If the mayonnaise is too thick, add a drop or two of water and process to mix.

To make by hand: Follow the directions for the machine method, using a bowl and whisk.

Place a dampened kitchen towel under the bowl to keep it from traveling while you whisk.

Should the mayonnaise curdle, all is not lost. Place ½ teaspoon Dijon mustard in a clean bowl. Stir 1 tablespoon at a time of the curdled mixture into the bowl with the mustard, whisking vigorously after each addition. You can use a handheld mixer for this process. You should have a nice stiff mayonnaise at the end. Be sure to go slowly at first so that the emulsifying, or thickening, can start.

Roasting Peppers

Roasted peppers are a delicious and eye-catching addition to a salad. Their vibrant color and fire-roasted taste add a new dimension to many dishes. Although they are now readily available in supermarkets, they are easy and economical to prepare at home.

To roast peppers, preheat the broiler. Halve the peppers lengthwise and remove the stem, seeds, and ribs. Place the pepper halves, cut side down, on a baking sheet lined with aluminum foil. Broil until the skins of the peppers are blackened and blistered all over. Alternatively, if you have a gas stove, leave the peppers whole and spear them one at a time on a long fork. Char the pepper directly over the open flame, turning it to blacken and blister evenly.

Transfer the blackened peppers to a paper or a plastic bag, close the bag, and let stand for about 10 minutes. Remove the peppers from the bag and peel away the charred skin. Use as directed in the recipe.

After they have cooled, store roasted peppers wrapped in plastic wrap for up to 2 days. Alternatively, they may be placed in a container, covered with olive oil, and stored in the refrigerator, covered, for up to 1 week.

Good-quality roasted peppers in jars are available in most supermarkets. You may also find them sold in bulk in Italian groceries. One 7- to 8-ounce bell pepper, roasted, is the equivalent of ¾ cup (4½ ounces) commercially roasted peppers.

Blanching Vegetables

Blanching, or parboiling, is a technique used to retain the color and texture of vegetables, as well as removing skins from tomatoes and stone fruit such as peaches. The food is briefly submerged in boiling water, removed quickly, and drained. Sometimes it is then immediately plunged into a bowl of ice water or placed under cold running water to set the color and texture and prevent further cooking. If a vegetable is of a delicate structure, such as broccoli florets or slices of summer squash, remove from the boiling water gently with a slotted spoon, skip the water bath to avoid a soggy or mushy result, and let cool to room temperature.

To remove the skin from a tomato, place the tomato on the tines of a fork and plunge it into boiling water for 10 seconds. Remove it and, with a sharp knife, make an X in the bottom of the tomato. The skin should separate from the flesh. Peel away the skin and discard.

If a recipe calls for blanching vegetables, you can save time by bringing the pasta water to a boil, using it for the blanching, and then cooking the pasta in the same water. This eliminates the necessity of bringing two pots of water to a boil.

Toasting Nuts and Seeds

Although the nuts and seeds called for in most of the recipes in this book can be used as they come from the can or the bag, toasting them lends richness and develops their flavor. Unless the recipe specifies whole nuts, chop them *before* toasting, as the cut sides of the nuts allow the oils to come to the surface, resulting in more flavor.

You can toast nuts and seeds in a skillet on the stovetop or on a baking sheet in the oven. You can also microwave them, but I find this method tedious, as they must be turned every 30 to 40 seconds.

To toast nuts and seeds in a skillet (this works best for a small quantity, ½ cup or less): Warm the skillet over medium heat, add the nuts or seeds, and stir frequently until they begin to turn golden brown and fragrant, about 2 minutes. Remove from the heat and immediately transfer to a plate or bowl, as they will continue to brown if left in the skillet.

To toast nuts and seeds in the oven: Preheat the oven to 350°F. Spread the nuts or seeds on a baking sheet and toast in the oven until they begin to turn golden brown and fragrant, 6 to 8 minutes, checking them after about 3 minutes and stirring them at that time. Remove from the oven and transfer them immediately to a plate or bowl.

Whichever method you use, watch carefully, as the high fat content of both nuts and seeds causes them to go quickly from perfectly toasted to burned.

: vegetable pasta salad

Orecchiette and Roasted Butternut Squash with Honey-Ginger Dressing

In New England, we take our winter squash very seriously. Its appearance at the local farm stands along with the brilliant foliage signals the arrival of the first frosty nights and is a portent of the long winter to come. I love the nutty, mellow flavor of butternut squash, which in this recipe is further enhanced by roasting. The natural sweetness becomes more intense as the juices caramelize in the cooking process. Little round pillows of orecchiette are the ideal pasta to pair with the squash for this piquant side dish. If you cannot find orecchiette, fiori (flower-shaped) pasta is an excellent substitute.

NOTE *If time is an issue, butternut squash is available peeled and cubed in the produce section of many supermarkets.*

SERVES 6

- 2 tablespoons butter
- 2 tablespoons canola oil
- 1 butternut squash, 1¼ to 1½ pounds, peeled, seeded and cut into ½-inch chunks *(see Note)*
- Salt and freshly ground black pepper
- 8 ounces orecchiette or fiori
- ½ cup fresh cranberries, chopped

DRESSING

- ½ cup canola oil
- 2 tablespoons fresh lemon juice
- 1 teaspoon sugar
- Pinch of freshly ground black pepper
- Pinch of paprika
- Pinch of dry mustard
- ¼ cup honey
- 1 tablespoon peeled, minced fresh ginger

PREPARATION

Preheat the oven to 400°F.

Put the butter and the oil on a baking sheet and place in the oven. When the butter-oil mixture is melted, add the squash chunks to the sheet and toss to coat. Sprinkle with a little salt and pepper, toss again to coat, and roast for 10 minutes. Stir the squash; it should be beginning to brown. Roast 10 minutes longer and stir again. When the squash is tender but not mushy, remove and set aside. Total cooking time should be about 25 minutes.

Meanwhile, cook the pasta according to the directions on the package for al dente. Drain in a colander and rinse briefly under cold running water. Shake the colander gently to drain completely. Set aside.

To make the dressing, place the oil and lemon juice in a small bowl and add the sugar, pepper, paprika, and mustard. Whisk together until the sugar has dissolved. Add the honey and ginger and whisk again.

Place the pasta in a large serving bowl and add the roasted squash and the cranberries. Pour the dressing over the mixture and toss gently but thoroughly, being careful not to mash the squash chunks. Serve immediately, or cover and refrigerate for up to 8 hours. Return to room temperature before serving.

Spicy Soba Sesame Salad

Soba, or Japanese buckwheat noodles, have a distinctively nutty flavor
and a brownish-gray color. They are
made from buckwheat flour and should
have no other additives; be sure to
read the package. These noodles have
a coarser texture than their Italian
counterparts. They are readily found in
Asian supermarkets and are becoming
more available in the Asian section of
local supermarkets, as well. Cooked
shrimp or chicken may be added to this
tasty dish.

SERVES 6

○ 8 ounces soba noodles
○ 1 package *(10 ounces)* frozen snow peas, thawed, or 1 cup fresh, blanched *(see page 20)* snow peas, strings removed
○ 1 red bell pepper, seeded, deribbed, and cut into medium dice
○ 4 green onions, including tender green tops, thinly sliced
○ ¼ cup sesame seeds, toasted *(see page 21)*

DRESSING

○ 3 tablespoons seasoned rice wine vinegar
○ ¼ teaspoon red pepper flakes, or to taste
○ 1 tablespoon sesame oil
○ 1 teaspoon hot chile oil
○ 1 tablespoon tamari
○ ⅓ cup peanut oil

PREPARATION

Cook the soba noodles according to the directions on the package. Do not overcook. Drain in a colander and rinse briefly under cold running water. Shake the
colander gently to drain completely. Place the noodles in a large serving bowl.

To make the dressing, in a small bowl, whisk together the vinegar, red pepper
flakes, sesame oil, chile oil, and tamari. Slowly whisk in the peanut oil until an
emulsion forms.

Pour the dressing over the noodles. Add the snow peas, bell pepper, onions, and
sesame seeds. (If you are refrigerating the salad, do not add the snow peas until
just before serving, as the acid in the dressing will cause them to lose their brilliant green color.) Toss the mixture gently but thoroughly. Cover and refrigerate
for up to 24 hours, or serve at once.

Autumn Shells Salad with Curried Apples, Pears, and Walnuts

September is a glorious time in New England. The days are still warm, but the air is somehow softer, more mellow. The first crisp nights signal the arrival of local apples in a whole spectrum of bright reds and greens, tumbling out of their baskets at the farm stands. Accompanied by grilled sausages or a juicy pork tenderloin, this crunchy salad is a tasty addition to that first autumnal meal.

NOTE *If you do not wish to buy a whole pineapple, you may find precut (cored and sliced or chunked) fresh pineapple in the produce section of your local supermarket.*

SERVES 6

- 6 ounces small or medium shells
- 1 Red Delicious apple
- 1 Granny Smith apple
- 1 Anjou pear
- 2 tablespoons fresh lemon juice
- ¼ cup chopped celery
- 1 cup fresh pineapple chunks *(see Note)* or 1 can *(8 ounces)* pineapple chunks, well drained
- 2 tablespoons chopped fresh flat-leaf parsley
- 2 tablespoons chopped walnuts, toasted *(see page 21)*

DRESSING

- ½ cup mayonnaise, homemade *(page 19)* or high-quality purchased
- ¼ cup plain yogurt
- 1 tablespoon curry powder
- Salt and freshly ground pepper

PREPARATION

Cook the shells according to the directions on the package for al dente. Drain in a colander and rinse briefly under cold running water. Shake the colander gently to drain completely, making sure no water is trapped inside the shells. Set aside.

Core the apples and the pear, but do not peel. Cut into small dice, place in a bowl, and sprinkle with the lemon juice to prevent browning. Toss to coat.

To make the dressing, whisk together the mayonnaise, yogurt, and curry powder in a small bowl. Season with salt and pepper to taste.

In a large serving bowl, toss together the pasta, apples, pear, celery, pineapple, and parsley. Pour the dressing over the mixture and toss again, gently but thoroughly. If serving immediately, sprinkle the walnuts over the salad; or, reserve the walnuts, cover, and refrigerate for up to 8 hours. Sprinkle the walnuts over the salad just before serving.

Fusilli Salad with Sugar Snap Peas and Roasted Peppers

Sugar snap peas and the rare days of June are synonymous. When I see the sign advertising the arrival of fresh sugar snap peas at Moulton Farm, our local farm stand, I am a happy person. Nothing is quite like the first fresh, crunchy green sugar snap pea, bursting with flavor, popped into the mouth while driving home from the stand. The season is so short, I use them in as many ways as I can while I can. Combined with fusilli and the lush flavor of roasted peppers, the peas are a burst of color in this delicious salad.

SERVES 8

- 8 ounces fusilli
- 2 cups sugar snap peas, strings removed, blanched *(see page 20)* if desired
- 4 green onions, including tender green tops, thinly sliced
- 1 red bell pepper, roasted *(see page 20)* and cut into 1/4-inch strips
- 1 yellow bell pepper, roasted *(see page 20)* and cut into 1/4-inch strips

DRESSING

- 3 tablespoons rice wine vinegar
- 1 teaspoon sugar
- 1/2 teaspoon salt
- Freshly ground black pepper
- 1/3 cup extra-virgin olive oil
- 1/2 cup loosely packed basil leaves, cut into chiffonade *(see page 15)*

PREPARATION

Cook the fusilli according to the directions on the package for al dente. Drain in a colander and rinse briefly under cold running water. Shake the colander gently to drain completely. Set aside.

To make the dressing, in a small bowl, combine the vinegar, sugar, salt, and pepper to taste. Slowly whisk in the olive oil until an emulsion forms. Stir in the basil.

Place the pasta in a large serving bowl and add the sugar snap peas, green onions and pepper strips. (If you are refrigerating the salad, do not add the peas until just before serving, as the acid in the dressing will cause them to lose their brilliant green color.) Toss together gently. Pour the dressing over the mixture and toss again, gently but thoroughly. Serve immediately, or cover and refrigerate for up to 8 hours.

Greek Orzo Salad with Tomatoes and Cucumbers in Lemon Dressing

Ever since my first visit to Greece, I have been enchanted by all things Greek—the food, the people, the mythology, and the sparkling clarity of the islands. Once, in the seaside town of Piraeus, I was served a salad that was especially delicious. Maybe it was the setting, the brilliant azure water beyond the pier, or the company; for some reason the salad has remained in my memory. I have re-created it here and leave you to provide the scenery. The egg-and-lemon based dressing, known as *avgolemono,* is used as a finishing touch to many Greek dishes.

SERVES 6

○ 6 ounces orzo
○ 2 large ripe tomatoes, peeled *(see page 20)*, seeded *(see page 15)*, and diced
○ 1 cucumber, peeled, seeded, and chopped
○ 1 cup kalamata olives, pitted *(see page 15)* and chopped
○ 4 green onions, including tender green tops, thinly sliced
○ ½ cup crumbled feta cheese
○ 3 tablespoons minced fresh oregano or 1 tablespoon dried oregano, crumbled

DRESSING

○ 2 eggs
○ Zest and juice of 1 large lemon
○ ½ cup hot chicken stock
○ ¼ cup sour cream
○ Salt
○ ½ teaspoon freshly ground white or black pepper

PREPARATION

Cook the orzo according to the directions on the package for al dente. Drain in a colander and rinse briefly under cold running water. Shake the colander gently to drain completely. Set aside.

To make the dressing, in a small bowl, beat the eggs together with the lemon zest and juice. Place the mixture in a small saucepan over low heat. Gradually add the hot stock, stirring constantly, until all the stock is used. Continue stirring until the mixture thickens and coats the back of a spoon, 4 to 5 minutes. Transfer to a small bowl and set aside to cool. When the egg mixture is at room temperature, whisk in the sour cream. Add salt to taste and the pepper.

Place the pasta in a large salad bowl and add the tomatoes, cucumber, olives, green onions, feta, and oregano. Toss together gently. Pour the cooled dressing over the mixture and toss again, gently but thoroughly. Serve immediately, or cover and refrigerate for up to 24 hours. Bring to room temperature before serving.

B & B Fusilli Salad with Goat Cheese and Arugula

I operated my home in New Hampshire as a bed-and-breakfast for eleven years. Many of my guests were regulars, coming at the same time each year for boating, fishing, or family get-togethers. Occasionally guests would ask me to put a picnic lunch together for them. When my garden was lush with tiny arugula leaves, this salad was included. The pleasantly pungent taste of creamy goat cheese combines with the peppery zing of the baby arugula leaves to produce a delectable medley of sharp and sweet. If you cannot find small arugula leaves, you may substitute baby spinach leaves; the salad will have a milder flavor.

SERVES 6

- 8 ounces fusilli
- ½ cup oil-packed sun-dried tomatoes, drained with 1 tablespoon oil reserved, sliced
- 4 ounces chilled goat cheese, crumbled
- 2 cups baby arugula leaves, coarsely chopped
- ½ cup niçoise olives, pitted *(see page 15)* and coarsely chopped

DRESSING

- 3 tablespoons red wine vinegar
- 1 shallot, minced
- ½ teaspoon freshly ground black pepper
- ½ cup extra-virgin olive oil

PREPARATION

Cook the fusilli according to the directions on the package for al dente. Drain in a colander and rinse briefly under cold running water. Toss with the reserved 1 tablespoon reserved tomato oil. Set aside.

To make the dressing, in a small bowl, whisk together the vinegar, shallot, and pepper. Add the olive oil gradually, whisking until an emulsion forms

Place the fusilli in a large serving bowl. Add the goat cheese, arugula, olives, and sun-dried tomatoes. Toss together gently. Pour the dressing over the mixture and toss again, gently but thoroughly. Serve immediately, or cover and refrigerate for up to 8 hours.

Cellentani Salad with Baby Peas and Mint

I have a passion for peas, particularly the first of the season. If I am fortunate enough to be in Italy in the spring, I buy them by the kilo, and can make an entire meal of them. Italians sometimes combine the peas with small chunks of prosciutto or *prosciutto cotto* (boiled ham) and cook them briefly with just a little onion and butter and a dash of salt and pepper for seasoning. In this salad, I've combined a medley of spring-time flavors that will tempt the most jaded palate of winter. Mint, growing wild by the roadside or picked from the garden, is a piquant addition to the dressing. You may omit the ham for a delicious vegetarian salad, if you wish.

SERVES 6 TO 8

- 8 ounces cellentani
- 1 pound fresh peas, shelled to equal about 1⅓ cups, blanched *(see page 20)*, or 1 package *(10 ounces)* frozen baby peas, thawed
- ½ pound fresh asparagus, trimmed, blanched *(see page 20)*, and cut into ½-inch pieces
- ¼ cup thinly sliced green onions, including tender green tops
- ¼ pound boiled ham or prosciutto, cut into ¼-inch dice
- ½ cup thinly sliced radishes
- ½ cup finely chopped fresh flat-leaf parsley
- Fresh mint sprigs for garnish *(optional)*

DRESSING

- ¼ cup rice wine vinegar
- 1 clove garlic, minced
- 1 shallot, minced
- 2 teaspoons Dijon mustard
- Salt and freshly ground black pepper
- ½ cup grapeseed or canola oil
- ½ cup finely chopped fresh mint

PREPARATION

Cook the cellentani according to the directions on the package for al dente. Drain in a colander and rinse briefly under cold running water. Shake the colander gently to drain completely. Set aside.

To make the dressing, in a small bowl, whisk together the vinegar, garlic, shallot, mustard, and salt and pepper to taste. Add the oil gradually, whisking until an emulsion forms. Stir in the chopped mint.

Place the pasta in a large serving bowl and add the peas, asparagus, green onions, ham, radishes, and parsley. Toss together gently. Pour the dressing over the mixture and toss again, gently but thoroughly. Serve immediately, or cover and refrigerate for up to 8 hours. Garnish with the mint sprigs, if using, at serving time.

Fettuccine with a Trio of Tomatoes Salad

One July I traveled to New Jersey to help with my then five-year-old grandson Jake, at the time of the birth of his brother, Sam. My son, CH, and his wife, Lisa, are ardent gardeners, and the patch of tomatoes growing in their backyard truly gave credence to New Jersey's name as "The Garden State." They had Romas, San Remos, Beefsteaks, heirlooms such as Striped German and Hillbilly, and grape cherry tomatoes, all hanging heavily on the vine, ripe for the picking. The shiny red globes were bursting with flavor and gave off that deliciously pungent smell that only very fresh tomatoes can. I served this salad one warm evening to tempt the new mother's appetite. In this recipe, really fresh, ripe tomatoes are the key to success. A good crusty loaf of bread to mop up the juices is a nice accompaniment.

SERVES 4 TO 6

- 8 ounces fettuccine
- 1 cup grape or cherry tomatoes, halved
- 2 large tomatoes such as Beefsteak or one of the heirlooms, peeled *(see page 20)* and cut into chunks
- 4 Roma *(plum)* tomatoes, peeled *(see page 20)*, seeded *(see page 15)*, and diced
- 1 large red onion, halved and thinly sliced
- 1 tablespoon capers, drained
- ½ cup chopped fresh oregano leaves
- Fresh oregano sprigs for garnish *(optional)*
- Freshly grated Parmesan cheese for serving

DRESSING

- 3 tablespoons red wine vinegar
- 1 teaspoon sugar
- ½ teaspoon salt
- Freshly ground black pepper
- ⅓ cup extra-virgin olive oil

PREPARATION

Cook the fettuccine according to the recipe on the package for al dente. Drain in a colander and rinse briefly under cold running water. Shake the colander gently to drain completely. Set aside.

To make the dressing, in a small bowl, combine the vinegar, sugar, salt, and pepper to taste. Whisk until the sugar and salt have dissolved, then whisk in the olive oil slowly until an emulsion forms.

Place the pasta in a large serving bowl. Place all the tomatoes, the onion, capers, and oregano in a bowl and add the dressing. Toss gently but thoroughly. Pour the tomato mixture on top of the pasta. Garnish with the sprigs of oregano, if using. Serve immediately, accompanied by the Parmesan, or cover and refrigerate for up to 8 hours.

Basket Makers' Shells and Mango Salad with Jicama and Celery Seed Dressing

My friend Liz Lapham, a very talented basket maker, teaches her craft in her studio in Meredith, New Hampshire. We teamed up and designed a class called "A Day of Country Arts," where the students learned how to weave a beautiful basket from Liz and had a cooking lesson from me, followed by lunch. They started in the morning working on their baskets and then adjourned from the studio to the kitchen, where I gave a demonstration of this flavorful salad. The students enjoyed the crunchy texture and sweet flavor of the salad for lunch, then finished their baskets and left with several new skills learned. It was a fun day for all! This salad also makes a nice addition to a brunch menu.

NOTE *Jicama is a bulbous root vegetable that generally comes from Mexico and South America. It should be peeled, and then may be served raw, or steamed, boiled, or baked. The white flesh of jicama has a sweet, nutty taste and crunchy texture. You may substitute water chestnuts if jicama is unavailable.*

SERVES 6

○ 8 ounces medium shells
○ 2 ripe mangoes, peeled and cut into ½-inch cubes
○ 1 cup peeled, diced jicama *(see Note)*
○ 1 cup red seedless grapes, halved

DRESSING

○ ¼ cup sugar
○ ¼ cup white wine vinegar
○ 1½ teaspoons dry mustard
○ ½ teaspoon salt
○ ¾ cup vegetable oil
○ 2 tablespoons celery seeds

PREPARATION

Cook the shells according to the directions on the package for al dente. Drain in a colander and rinse briefly under cold running water. Shake the colander gently to drain completely, making sure no water is trapped inside the shells. Set aside.

To make the dressing, combine the sugar, vinegar, mustard, and salt in a blender or a food processor. Process until mixed thoroughly, then add the oil and process until smooth. Add the celery seeds and pulse just to mix.

Place the pasta in a large serving bowl and add the mangoes, jicama, and grapes. Toss together gently. Add the dressing and toss again, gently but thoroughly. Serve immediately, or cover and refrigerate for up to 8 hours.

Radiatore Salad with Roasted Vegetables

I am completely enamored of roasted vegetables. The process of roasting a cut-up vegetable releases a most delicious, sweet taste as the juices and sugars within rise to the cut surfaces and caramelize. Just about any vegetable can be roasted; root vegetables are a favorite during our long New England winters. However, softer vegetables are equally delicious. Just as long as you choose vegetables somewhat similar in density, they will soften in roughly the same amount of time. Italians have been on to this method long before it became trendy here. I fell in love with the sweet taste of roasted fennel at the home of Italian friends years ago. Marcella Hazan's recipe for roasted mixed vegetables in her first book, *The Classic Italian Cookbook*, is a favorite in my cooking classes. In this recipe I have used eggplant, tomato, and fennel, but there are many other possibilities; the cooking time may vary slightly. This salad complements a grilled or roasted loin of pork very nicely.

SERVES 4 TO 6

- 1 zucchini, about 6 ounces, cut into ½-inch cubes
- ½ globe eggplant, cut into ½-inch cubes
- 4 Roma *(plum)* tomatoes, seeded *(see page 15)* and quartered
- ½ teaspoon salt
- ¼ teaspoon freshly ground black pepper
- 2 teaspoons chopped fresh thyme or 1 teaspoon dried thyme, crumbled
- ¼ cup extra-virgin olive oil
- 8 ounces radiatore
- ¼ cup freshly grated Parmesan cheese
- ⅓ cup pine nuts, toasted *(see page 21)*

DRESSING

- 4 tablespoons red wine vinegar
- 2 teaspoons Dijon mustard
- Salt and freshly ground black pepper
- ½ cup extra-virgin olive oil

PREPARATION

Preheat the oven to 425°F.

Place the zucchini, eggplant, and tomatoes in a bowl. Add the salt, pepper, and thyme. Pour the olive oil over the vegetables and toss well so that all the vegetables are coated. Arrange the vegetables on a baking sheet in a single layer and bake for 10 minutes. Turn the vegetables and continue roasting until they are easily pierced with the tip of a knife, about 10 minutes longer. Set aside and let cool to room temperature.

While the vegetables are roasting, cook the radiatore according to the directions on the package for al dente. Drain in a colander and rinse briefly under cold running water. Shake the colander gently to drain completely. Set aside.

To make the dressing, in a small bowl whisk together the vinegar, mustard, and salt and pepper to taste. Slowly whisk in the olive oil until an emulsion forms.

Place the pasta in a large serving bowl and add the roasted vegetables, scraping any bits of charred vegetable from the baking sheet into the bowl as well. Toss together gently. Pour the dressing over the pasta and vegetables and toss again gently but thoroughly. Sprinkle the Parmesan and pine nuts over the top. Serve at once or cover and refrigerate for up to 8 hours. Bring the salad to room temperature before serving.

Couscous Vegetable Salad with Lemon Dressing

You may not think of couscous as a pasta, but according to *The Food Lover's Companion* by the talented teacher and author Sharon Tyler Herbst, it is "a granular semolina" found most often in North African cuisine. Semolina is derived by grinding durum wheat; the flour form is used in the manufacture of all commercial Italian pasta. You may purchase couscous in many flavors at the local supermarket, in a convenient instant form. This simple, refreshing salad takes minutes to make and holds up well in the refrigerator. Try varying this recipe with different flavors of couscous and a variety of vegetables. Think outside the box!

- 1 package *(10 ounces)* plain couscous
- 2 cups chicken broth
- 1 cup arugula leaves, cut into chiffonade *(see page 15)*
- 2 ripe tomatoes, peeled *(see page 20)*, seeded *(see page 15)*, and chopped
- 1 small cucumber, peeled, seeded, and diced
- 1 carrot, peeled and diced
- ½ cup kalamata olives, pitted *(see page 15)* and chopped
- ½ red onion, thinly sliced
- ½ cup chopped fresh flat-leaf parsley

DRESSING

- 3 tablespoons fresh lemon juice
- ½ teaspoon salt
- Freshly ground black pepper
- ⅓ cup extra-virgin olive oil

PREPARATION

Cook the couscous according to the directions on the package, using the chicken broth as the liquid. Fluff the couscous with a fork and place it in a large serving bowl. Add the arugula, tomatoes, cucumber, carrot, olives, onion, and parsley. Toss gently but thoroughly.

To make the dressing, place the lemon juice in a small bowl. Add the salt and pepper to taste and whisk together. Gradually add the olive oil and whisk until an emulsion forms.

Pour the dressing over the couscous mixture and toss gently but thoroughly. Serve immediately, or cover and refrigerate for up to 8 hours. This salad will keep for up to 24 hours, but more dressing may be required, as couscous tends to absorb dressing at a greater rate than other pasta.

Orzo Primavera Salad

Primavera, or springtime in Italy, can be magical. I have been fortunate enough to be in Cortona, in southern Tuscany, for several springs. The earth sends forth the first tender shoots of asparagus, tiny emerald peas grace the market stalls, and the miracle of the seasons is never felt more strongly. While at the market one morning, I was inspired to put together a salad of the primavera vegetables, based on the venerable *pasta primavera* found on many restaurant menus in the United States. Do not be limited by this recipe; choose whatever fresh spring vegetables are available in your market. The zesty taste of lemon in the dressing complements the freshness of the vegetables, but do not add the dressing until ready to serve, as the acid in the lemon will discolor the green vegetables.

- 8 ounces orzo
- ½ pound fresh young asparagus spears, blanched *(see page 20)* and cut into ½-inch pieces
- 1 cup baby peas, blanched *(see page 20)* if fresh, thawed if frozen
- ½ cup diced zucchini, blanched *(see page 20)*
- ½ cup diced carrots, blanched *(see page 20)*
- ½ cup thinly sliced radishes
- ¼ cup chopped red onion

DRESSING

- ¼ cup fresh lemon juice
- 1½ teaspoons grated lemon zest
- 1 clove garlic, minced
- Salt and freshly ground black pepper
- ½ cup extra-virgin olive oil
- ¼ cup loosely packed fresh basil leaves, cut into chiffonade *(see page 15)*

43

PREPARATION

Cook the orzo according to the directions on the package for al dente. Drain in a colander and rinse briefly under cold running water. Shake the colander gently to drain completely. Set aside.

To make the dressing, in a small bowl, whisk together the lemon juice and zest, garlic, and salt and pepper to taste. Gradually whisk in the olive oil until an emulsion forms. Stir in the basil.

Place the orzo in a large serving bowl and add the asparagus, peas, zucchini, carrots, radishes, and onion. Toss together gently. If serving immediately, add the dressing and toss again, gently but thoroughly, or, cover and refrigerate for up to 8 hours, and add the dressing just before serving.

Indian Summer Ravioli and Broccoli Salad

Labor Day has always been a bittersweet day for me. End of summer, end of carefree lazy afternoons at the lake, end of soft summer evenings listening to the town band at the gazebo, and the departure of the summer folk. It's a time to get serious, think of schedules, shake out the winter clothes and air them on the line. Time to order wood for the woodstove and put the garden to bed. But it is also a very special time, those few weeks in September and early October. The days are mellow, the first leaves begin to turn; the roads are less crowded; in fact it's a perfect time for a last lakeside picnic. You can put this salad together quickly and set off for your favorite spot. Take time to enjoy one last brief moment of Indian summer. Bring to room temperature before serving.

SERVES 6

- 1 package *(9 ounces)* cheese ravioli
- 1 small bunch broccoli, about 1 pound
- 1 red bell pepper, roasted *(see page 20)* and cut into ¼-inch strips
- 1 yellow bell pepper, roasted *(see page 20)* and cut into ¼-inch strips
- ½ cup thinly sliced green onions, including tender green tops
- 2 tablespoons capers, drained
- ½ cup loosely packed basil leaves, cut into chiffonade *(see page 15)* for garnish

DRESSING

- ¼ cup fresh lemon juice
- 1 clove garlic, minced
- ¼ cup chopped green onions, including tender green tops
- 1 tablespoon whole-grain Dijon mustard
- Salt and freshly ground black pepper
- 6 tablespoons extra-virgin olive oil
- ¼ cup minced fresh chives

PREPARATION

Cook the ravioli according to the directions on the package for al dente. Drain in a colander and rinse briefly with cold running water. Shake the colander gently to drain completely. Set aside.

While the pasta is cooking, remove the florets from the broccoli and thinly slice the tops of the stems, discarding the tough bottom ends. Blanch the florets and tender stems (page 20). Using a slotted spoon, transfer the broccoli to paper towels to drain thoroughly.

To make the dressing, in a small bowl, whisk together the lemon juice, garlic, green onions, mustard, and salt and pepper to taste. Slowly whisk in the olive oil until an emulsion is formed. Stir in the chives.

Put the pasta in a large serving bowl and add the blanched broccoli, the bell pepper strips, green onions, and capers. Toss together gently. Pour the dressing over the mixture and toss again, gently but thoroughly. Garnish with the basil strips. Serve immediately or cover and refrigerate for up to 1 hour.

Peaches and Pasta
Salad with Mint Pesto

Summer evenings on our screened porch are special times. The air is gentle and nature's orchestra, the peepers, punctuates the velvet night, tuning up for their evening concert. No need for scented candles here; the fragrance of the herbs from the nearby garden permeates the air. A relaxed evening is in store when preparations for the meal have been made early in the day. We light up the grill, put on some succulent spareribs or perhaps an herb-marinated butterflied leg of lamb, and assemble this refreshing and cool salad. Pesto made with mint from the garden complements the juicy morsels of meat. Only fresh mint will do here, but I have used frozen or high-quality canned peaches with success.

SERVES 6

○ 8 ounces small shells
○ 4 ripe peaches, blanched and skinned *(see page 20)*, or 2 cups frozen or high-quality canned peaches, thawed if frozen

PESTO

○ 2 cups firmly packed fresh mint leaves
○ ½ cup sugar
○ 2 tablespoons canola or grapeseed oil
○ 4 tablespoons balsamic vinegar
○ ¼ teaspoon freshly ground black pepper

PREPARATION

Cook the pasta according to the directions on the package for al dente. Drain in a colander and rinse briefly under cold running water. Shake the colander gently to drain completely. Set aside.

To make the pesto, combine the mint and sugar in a blender or food processor. Process until the mint is finely chopped. Add the oil, vinegar, and pepper and process until well blended.

Cut the peaches up into small chunks. Place the pasta in a large, shallow bowl and add the peaches. Toss together gently. Pour the mint pesto over the pasta mixture and toss again, gently but thoroughly. Serve immediately, or cover and refrigerate for up to 2 hours. The pasta in this salad will darken as it sits, due to the vinegar, so don't make it too far in advance.

Orecchiette Salad with Roasted Corn and Red Pepper

The Sandwich Fair, held in Center Sandwich, New Hampshire, every Columbus Day weekend, is the last country fair of the season in New England. It is truly a country fair, with oxen and tractor pulls and judging of cattle, sheep, and goats. There are exhibits of the last of summer's bounty, including the largest pumpkin grown, as well as glistening jars of homemade preserves and pickles. There is also a midway with rides and games and a wonderful parade. We have attended when it's been shirtsleeve weather, as well as when the trumpet players in the band had trouble blowing their horns due to the cold, as they marched along through blinding snow flurries. My children and grandchildren return from afar for the event. A simple supper at home follows the filling fair food of the day. Although our corn season is long finished by October, this salad can be made out of season with frozen corn, which roasts well. Grilled sausages make a nice accompaniment.

SERVES 6

◦ 8 ounces orecchiette
◦ 5 to 6 ears of corn, grilled with husks on, or 2 cups frozen corn, thawed
◦ 1 tablespoon olive oil, if using frozen corn
◦ 1 cup drained and rinsed canned garbanzo beans
◦ 1 red bell pepper, roasted *(see page 20)* and diced
◦ ⅓ cup minced fresh flat-leaf parsley

DRESSING

◦ 3 tablespoons red wine vinegar
◦ 2 cloves garlic, minced
◦ Salt and freshly ground black pepper
◦ ⅓ cup grapeseed or corn oil

PREPARATION

If using frozen corn, preheat the oven to 400°F.

Cook the orecchiette according to the directions on the package for al dente. Drain in a colander and rinse briefly under cold running water. Shake the colander gentl to drain completely. Set aside.

If you grilled the corn, after it is grilled, remove the husks and cut the kernels off the cob with a sharp knife. You should have about 2 cups. If using frozen corn, spread the thawed corn on a baking sheet, sprinkle the olive oil over it, and stir to coat. Roast, stirring every 5 minutes, until the corn is slightly browned and crunchy to the taste, about 15 minutes.

To make the dressing, in a small bowl, whisk together the vinegar, garlic, and salt and pepper to taste. Add the oil gradually, whisking until an emulsion forms.

Place the pasta in a large serving bowl and add the roasted corn, garbanzo beans roasted bell pepper, and parsley. Toss together gently. Pour the dressing over the mixture and toss again, gently but thoroughly. Serve immediately, or cover and refrigerate for up to 8 hours. Bring to room temperature before serving.

"Meredith in Bloom" Picnic Pasta Salad with Roasted Asparagus

- 2 tablespoons olive oil
- ½ pound fresh asparagus
- 1 tablespoon balsamic vinegar
- ½ teaspoon salt
- 8 ounces penne
- 1 cup oil-packed artichoke hearts, drained, 1 tablespoon oil reserved
- 2 cups fresh baby spinach leaves, torn if large
- 2 cups fresh white mushrooms, thinly sliced
- ¼ cup thinly sliced green onions, including tender green tops
- ¼ cup finely chopped fresh flat-leaf parsley
- ½ cup loosely packed fresh basil leaves, cut into chiffonade *(see page 15)*, for garnish

DRESSING

- 3 tablespoons rice wine vinegar
- 1 clove garlic, minced
- Salt and freshly ground black pepper
- ½ cup extra-virgin olive oil
- 1 tablespoon chopped fresh basil

In what has become an annual rite of spring, on a Saturday in mid-May, the town of Meredith, New Hampshire, celebrates "Meredith in Bloom." The event is held in a beautiful park on the shores of Lake Winnipesaukee. Sponsored by the town and a local bank and garden club, as well as Mill Falls Inns and Marketplace, the event is dedicated to the beautification of the village of Meredith by planting thousands of bulbs and flowering shrubs over a five-year period. There is live entertainment, horse and wagon rides, and the "Picnic in the Park" competition, where picnics are judged on presentation, theme, and creativity. My walking group won first prize several years ago with our entry. Against a backdrop of brilliant blue lake and sky, with a host of yellow daffodils swaying in the breeze, we spread our feast before the judges. Who could resist this fresh springtime pasta salad?

PREPARATION

Preheat the oven to 400°F. Brush a baking sheet with 1 tablespoon of the olive oil. Trim the ends of the asparagus, place them on the sheet, and turn to coat with the oil. Roast until the tip of a knife easily pierces the thickest stalk, 5 to 8 minutes. Transfer to a cutting board and cut into 2-inch lengths, then place on a platter. Add the remaining 1 tablespoon olive oil, the balsamic vinegar, and salt, and toss gently. If you are preparing ahead of time, cover the platter and marinate at room temperature for several hours.

While the asparagus is roasting, cook the penne according to the directions on the package for al dente. Drain in a colander and rinse briefly under cold running water. Shake the colander gently to drain completely. Toss with the 1 tablespoon reserved artichoke oil. Set aside. Cut the artichoke hearts in half. Set aside.

To make the dressing, in a small bowl, whisk together the vinegar, garlic, and salt and pepper to taste. Add the extra-virgin olive oil gradually, whisking until an emulsion forms. Stir in the chopped basil.

Place the pasta in a large serving bowl. Add the roasted asparagus, spinach, mushrooms, artichoke hearts, green onions, and parsley. Toss together gently. Pour the dressing over the mixture and toss again, gently but thoroughly. Garnish with the basil strips at serving time. Serve immediately, or cover and refrigerate for up to 8 hours.

Gemelli Crunchy Slaw

A brand new twist on the venerable favorite coleslaw, this salad's crunchy texture and piquant flavors will make it a standout at any event. The gemelli, or "twins," pasta shape combines well with the shredded cabbage. Pair the salad with slices of juicy tomatoes, plump hamburgers right off the grill, and you have a delicious meal.

NOTES *If time is an issue, there are several good quality bottled coleslaw dressings available at the supermarket. Use a proportionate amount to the recipe, about 1½ cups. Follow the directions for chilling. You can also save time by purchasing a 16-ounce package of preshredded coleslaw, which contains both cabbage and carrots.*

SERVES 6 TO 8

- 6 ounces gemelli
- 6 cups shredded green cabbage *(see Notes)*
- 1 large carrot, peeled and grated (if not using packaged slaw)
- ½ cup chopped walnuts, toasted *(see page 21)*
- ½ cup golden raisins
- ½ cup crumbled blue cheese

DRESSING *(see Notes):*

- 1 cup mayonnaise, homemade *(page 19)* or high-quality purchased
- ¼ cup sour cream
- 1 tablespoon minced red onion
- 1 tablespoon white balsamic vinegar
- 2 teaspoons Dijon mustard
- Salt and freshly ground pepper

PREPARATION

Cook the gemelli according to the directions on the box for al dente. Drain it in a colander and rinse briefly under cold running water. Shake the colander gently to drain completely. Set aside.

To make the dressing, whisk together the mayonnaise, sour cream, onion, vinegar, mustard, salt and pepper to taste in a small bowl.

Place the pasta in a large serving bowl and add the cabbage, carrot, walnuts, raisins, and blue cheese. Toss together gently.

Pour the dressing over the mixture and toss again, gently but thoroughly. Cover and refrigerate for at least 2 hours or up to 12 hours. Toss gently again before serving.

CHAPTER 4 : meat and poultry pasta salad

Radiatore Beef Salad with Horseradish Dressing

If you find yourself, as I often do, left with a nice piece of cold steak after a cookout, this salad is a delicious way to stretch that morsel of meat into a satisfying meal for several people. You may, of course, grill a steak just for the recipe. I like the curly shape of radiatore for this salad. It's a hearty dish, and offers a tempting change for the meat-and-potatoes crowd. Round out the meal with a crisp green salad, crusty bread, and a mellow glass of Merlot. Be sure to use recently purchased horseradish, as it loses its punch over time.

SERVES 6

- 8 ounces radiatori
- ½ pound cooked beef sirloin, cut into ½-inch cubes *(see Notes)*
- ¼ cup finely chopped red onion
- 1 cup grape or cherry tomatoes, halved
- ½ cup chopped celery
- 2 tablespoons chopped fresh flat-leaf parsley
- ½ cup crumbled blue cheese for garnish

DRESSING

- ⅓ cup mayonnaise, homemade *(page 19)* or high-quality purchased
- ⅓ cup sour cream
- ⅓ cup buttermilk *(see Notes)*
- 2 cloves garlic, minced
- 2 teaspoons Dijon mustard
- 1½ tablespoons prepared horseradish, drained
- Salt and freshly ground black pepper

PREPARATION

Cook the radiatore according to the directions on the package for al dente. Drain in a colander and rinse briefly under cold running water. Shake the colander gently to drain completely. Set aside.

To make the dressing, combine the mayonnaise, sour cream, and buttermilk in a small bowl. Whisk in the garlic, mustard, horseradish, and salt and pepper to taste.

Place the pasta in a large serving bowl and add the steak, onion, tomatoes, celery, and parsley. Toss together gently. Pour the dressing over the mixture and toss again, gently but thoroughly. Cover and refrigerate for at least 1 hour and up to 24 hours. Garnish with the blue cheese just before serving.

Annual Meeting Tortellini and Prosciutto Salad

Trinity Church in Meredith, New Hampshire, doubles its congregation in the summer months, due to its proximity to Lake Winnipesaukee and Squam Lake, of *On Golden Pond* fame. Because of this there are two Annual Meetings, so that both the summer and winter congregations can be involved. These meetings are followed by a potluck meal, where members of the church contribute delicious dishes. It always works out that there are a variety of delicious casseroles, salads, and desserts, with more than enough for everyone. This salad works nicely for a potluck, as it travels well and is served at room temperature. You may use any combination of packaged tortellini; there are often several choices of stuffing available. Ask the deli person to cut the prosciutto thicker than the usual paper-thin slices, so you can dice it.

SERVES 8 TO 10

- 1 package *(9 ounces)* spinach tortellini
- 1 package *(9 ounces)* cheese tortellini
- ½ cup oil-packed sun-dried tomatoes, drained and sliced, 1 tablespoon of oil reserved
- 4 ounces prosciutto, cut into ¼ inch dice
- ⅓ cup chopped red onion
- ⅓ cup minced fresh flat-leaf parsley

DRESSING

- 3 tablespoons red wine vinegar
- 1 tablespoon Dijon mustard
- 1 large clove garlic, minced
- ½ teaspoon red pepper flakes
- 1 tablespoon chopped fresh rosemary or 1 teaspoon dried rosemary, crumbled
- Salt and freshly ground black pepper
- ½ cup extra-virgin olive oil

PREPARATION

Cook the tortellini according to the instructions on the package for al dente. Drain in a colander and rinse briefly under cold running water. Shake the colander gently to drain completely. Toss carefully with the reserved tomato oil. Set aside.

To make the dressing, in a small bowl, whisk together the vinegar, mustard, garlic, pepper flakes, rosemary, and salt and black pepper to taste. Whisk in the olive oil gradually until an emulsion forms.

Place the tortellini in a large serving bowl. Add the prosciutto, onion, sun-dried tomatoes, and parsley. Toss together gently. Pour the dressing over the mixture and toss again, gently but thoroughly. Serve immediately, or cover and refrigerate for up to 8 hours.

Chicken Rigatoni Caesar Salad

New Hampshire folk take their politics very seriously. The state's motto is "Live Free or Die," and the first in the nation status of the presidential primary is hotly defended. I serve as a ballot clerk for our local and national primaries and elections. Aside from clerking, I provide the poll workers' evening meal. I thoroughly enjoy the challenge of this, as there are many different taste buds involved, the time for eating is short (before they count the ballots), and the dish must be able to wait around! My collection of Election Day recipes includes this salad that fits these requirements.

SERVES 8

- 8 ounces mini rigatoni
- 2 cups cooked, cubed chicken
- ⅔ cup finely chopped red onion
- ½ cup chopped flat-leaf parsley
- 1 cup freshly grated Parmesan cheese
- Romaine lettuce leaves
- 1 cup herb-flavored croutons, crumbled for garnish
- 8 rolled anchovy fillets with capers, drained and blotted dry *(optional)*

DRESSING

- ¼ cup fresh lemon juice
- 2 teaspoons Worcestershire sauce
- 2 cloves garlic, minced
- 1 teaspoon dry mustard
- Salt and freshly ground black pepper to taste
- 1 teaspoon anchovy paste *(optional)*
- ⅔ cup extra-virgin olive oil

PREPARATION

Cook the pasta according to the directions on the box for al dente. Drain it into a colander and rinse briefly under cold running water. Shake the colander gently to drain completely. Set aside.

To make the dressing, in a small bowl whisk together the lemon juice, Worcestershire sauce, garlic, dry mustard, salt and pepper, and anchovy paste, if using, until incorporated. Slowly whisk in the olive oil, forming an emulsion.

Place the pasta in a large bowl and add the chicken cubes, onion, parsley and cheese. Toss gently. Pour the dressing over the mixture and toss again, gently but thoroughly. Cover and refrigerate for 1 hour, or up to 8 hours.

Just before serving, line a serving platter with romaine leaves. Place the salad on the leaves, and sprinkle the croutons over it. Garnish with optional anchovy fillets.

Pipette Salad
with Ham and Eggs

Pipette, or "little pipes," a relatively new pasta to arrive in this country, is a wonderful shape for a salad with a creamy dressing. Kin to the venerable elbow macaroni, their little curves trap the tangy dressing and complement the dice of ham and egg in this recipe. This salad makes a nice addition to a potluck meal. If you are unable to find the pipettes, mini rigatoni or elbows will work well. If you are buying your ham from the deli counter, ask for it to be cut in one or two thick slices so that you will be able to cut it into a nice dice. Try filling a hollowed-out juicy, ripe tomato with this salad: It makes a lovely presentation.

SERVES 6 TO 8

- 8 ounces pipette
- 1½ cups diced baked ham, about 6 ounces
- 3 hard-boiled eggs, chopped
- ½ cup green bell pepper, seeded, deribbed, and diced
- ⅓ cup chopped red onion
- ⅓ cup chopped celery

DRESSING

- ½ cup mayonnaise, homemade *(page 19)* or high-quality purchased
- ½ cup plain yogurt
- 2 teaspoons Dijon mustard
- Salt and freshly ground black pepper
- ¼ cup sweet pickle relish, drained

PREPARATION

Cook the pipette according to the directions on the package for al dente. Drain in a colander and rinse briefly under cold running water. Shake the colander gently to drain completely. Set aside.

To make the dressing, in a small bowl, whisk together the mayonnaise, yogurt, mustard, and salt and pepper to taste. Fold in the pickle relish.

Place the pasta in a large serving bowl and add the ham, eggs, bell pepper, onion, and celery. Pour the dressing over the mixture and toss gently but thoroughly. Cover and refrigerate for at least 1 hour and up to 8 hours.

Pepperoni Pizza Salad

Who doesn't like pizza? When dealing with America's favorite fast food, fans generally fall into two camps. Whether you are a fan of the deep-dish, thick-crusted variety or prefer a thin, crispy, crunchy texture, the appeal of the famous Italian pie is universal. This salad combines some of the more popular pizza flavors with pasta, resulting in a colorful dish bursting with taste, fit to bring to any gathering. If you customarily say "hold the anchovies" when ordering pizza, try using the small amount of anchovy paste called for in this recipe anyway. Believe me, you do not taste it; it just lends a subtle flavor to the final result.

- 8 ounces ditalini or other small, tubular pasta
- 4 ounces pepperoni sausage, cut into ¼-slices, then the slices quartered
- ½ cup green bell pepper, seeded, deribbed and chopped
- 2 ripe tomatoes, peeled *(see page 20)* and cut into bite-sized chunks
- 1 cup fresh white mushrooms, thinly sliced
- ½ cup pitted black olives, thinly sliced
- 8 ounces mozzarella, shredded

DRESSING

- 3 tablespoons red wine vinegar
- Salt and freshly ground black pepper
- 1 teaspoon anchovy paste *(optional)*
- 1 clove garlic, minced
- 2 teaspoons dried oregano, crumbled
- ⅓ cup extra-virgin olive oil

PREPARATION

Cook the pasta according to the directions on the package for al dente. Drain into a colander and rinse briefly under cold running water. Shake the colander gently to drain completely. Set aside.

To make the dressing, in a small bowl, whisk together the vinegar and salt and pepper to taste. Whisk in the anchovy paste, if using, garlic, and oregano. Slowly whisk in the olive oil until an emulsion forms.

Place the pasta, pepperoni, bell pepper, tomatoes, mushrooms, olives, and mozzarella in a large serving bowl. Toss together gently. Pour the dressing over the mixture and toss again, gently but thoroughly. Serve immediately, or cover and refrigerate for up to 8 hours.

Chinese Chicken Salad with Rice Noodles

The kind of Chinese rice noodles that resemble fettuccini work well in this crisp salad bursting with flavor. These are also the noodles used for pad Thai. In this recipe, you may substitute shrimp for the chicken, if you wish. I served this salad to my walking group one day, after a vigorous hike up and down the hills of Meredith, New Hampshire. It received rave reviews. I was able to make it ahead and produce it out of the refrigerator when we returned. Try to find rice noodles that do not have added cornstarch in the ingredients.

NOTE *Tamari is a naturally brewed Japanese soy sauce, very dark, rich, and slightly thicker and less salty than Chinese soy sauce. It is available in the Asian section of most supermarkets.*

SERVES 6 TO 8

- 8 ounces Asian rice noodles *(see page 10)*
- 2 cups cooked, cubed chicken
- 6 green onions, including tender green tops, sliced, plus 2 green onions chopped fine for garnish
- 2 carrots, peeled and shredded
- 1 can *(8 ounces)* water chestnuts, drained and coarsely chopped
- ½ cup chopped unsalted peanuts

DRESSING

- 2 tablespoons seasoned rice wine vinegar
- ¼ cup tamari *(see Note)*
- 1 tablespoon honey
- 2 teaspoons chopped garlic
- ½ teaspoon peeled, chopped fresh ginger
- ¼ cup peanut oil

PREPARATION

Cook the noodles according to the directions on the package. Do not overcook. Drain in a colander and rinse briefly under cold running water. Shake the colander gently to drain completely. Set aside.

To make the dressing, in a small bowl, whisk together the vinegar, tamari, honey, garlic, and ginger. Slowly whisk in the oil until an emulsion forms.

Place the noodles, chicken, sliced green onions, carrots, and water chestnuts in a large serving bowl. Pour the dressing over the mixture and toss gently but thoroughly. Cover and refrigerate for at least 1 hour and up to 8 hours. Just before serving, toss again gently and garnish with the chopped peanuts and chopped green onions.

Snow Party Pasta Salad

Every year on the second weekend in February, the Great Rotary Ice Fishing Derby is held on Lake Winnipesaukee, in the Lakes Region of central New Hampshire. Out on the lake, a small village of "bob houses" springs up overnight. Local folk stroll out on the ice and enjoy the festivities and creative architecture of the bob houses. The derby provides an economic boost to the area in the low-tourist season while creating great opportunities for the local residents to socialize. Lydia and Nate Torrs' "Martinis in the Snow" party is a coveted invitation. Guests arrive on snowshoes, skis, or by auto at their lakeside cottage driveway, where Nate has submerged the adult beverages in the snowbanks to chill. The barbecue grill glows, and fragrant kettles of soup and stew simmer in slow cookers. I brought this hearty salad to the snow party one year, to add to the sumptuous feast.

NOTE *Chipotle chiles come canned in a smoky-flavored tomato sauce called adobo. They are available in most supermarkets or Latin American markets.*

- 8 ounces cellentani or other spiral pasta
- 1½ tablespoons extra-virgin olive oil
- ½ pound kielbasa sausage, cut into ¼-inch slices, then the slices halved
- 1 can *(15 ounces)* garbanzo beans, rinsed and drained
- 2 celery stalks, thinly sliced
- ½ cup green olives, pitted *(see page 15)* and chopped
- ¼ cup chopped red onion
- ½ cup finely chopped fresh flat-leaf parsley

DRESSING

- 1 chipotle chile in adobo sauce, stemmed, seeded, and chopped *(see Note)*
- 2 teaspoons adobo sauce from the can
- 3 tablespoons red wine vinegar
- Salt and freshly ground black pepper
- ½ cup extra-virgin olive oil

PREPARATION

Cook the pasta according to the directions on the package for al dente. Drain in a colander and rinse briefly under cold running water. Shake the colander gently to drain completely. Set aside.

In a skillet over medium heat, warm the 1½ tablespoons olive oil. Add the sausage pieces and sauté until lightly browned, about 4 minutes. Using a slotted spoon, transfer pieces to paper towels to drain.

To make the dressing, in a small bowl, stir together the chile and additional adobo sauce, the vinegar, and salt and pepper to taste. Gradually whisk in the ½ cup olive oil until an emulsion forms.

Place the pasta in a large serving bowl and add the drained sausage, garbanzo beans, celery, olives, onion, and parsley. Toss together gently. Pour the dressing over the mixture and toss again, gently but thoroughly. Serve immediately, or cover and refrigerate for up to 8 hours.

The Antipasto Salad

Antipasto literally means "before the meal," and is usually an assortment of cold, sometimes pickled, vegetables and cheese, olives, and meats or perhaps some seafood. There are no hard-and-fast rules for an antipasto platter assembly. This salad is a tossed version of an antipasto platter, with the addition of a pasta of your choice. I've given you some suggestions here as to the composition of an antipasto pasta salad, but the fun of this salad is creating your own signature dish. Raid your Italian grocery store for some unusual specialties such as pickled vegetables or bottled peppers stuffed with prosciutto. This salad multiplies easily to serve any number. Good bread to mop up the juices and a glass of Chianti will make this meal memorable.

SERVES 6 OR MORE

- 1 package *(9 ounces)* cheese tortellini
- 1 package *(9 ounces)* frozen artichoke hearts, thawed and quartered
- 1 jar *(6 ounces)* marinated mushrooms, drained, marinade reserved

Any of the following in ¼ - to ½-cup quantities:
- Sweet or hot cherry peppers, or a few of each, quartered
- Roasted red, green, or yellow bell peppers *(see page 20)* or bottled roasted red peppers, drained and sliced
- Pepperoncini peppers
- Black or green olives, pitted *(see page 15)* or a combination
- Pickled vegetables such as carrots or cauliflower
- Cubes of provolone or mozzarella
- Bocconcini *(little balls of fresh mozzarella marinated in olive oil)*
- Pepperoni, salami, capicola, or mortadella, cut into cubes *or* sardines, anchovy fillets, or Italian olive oil–packed tuna

DRESSING

- ¼ cup red wine vinegar
- 2 cloves garlic, minced
- 1 teaspoon dried oregano, crumbled
- Salt and freshly ground black pepper
- Reserved marinade from mushrooms *(above)* mixed with enough extra-virgin olive oil to equal ½ cup

PREPARATION

Cook the tortellini according to the directions on the package for al dente. Drain in a colander and rinse briefly under cold running water. Shake the colander gently to drain completely. Set aside.

To make the dressing, in a small bowl, whisk together the vinegar, garlic, oregano, and salt and pepper to taste. Whisk in the oil mixture gradually, whisking until an emulsion forms.

Place the pasta in a large serving bowl and add your selection of vegetables, cheese, and meat or fish. Toss together gently. Pour the dressing over the mixture and toss again, gently but thoroughly. Serve immediately, or cover and refrigerate for up to 8 hours.

Asian Peanut Noodles with Shredded Chicken

The Chinese people say that eating noodles is good luck because noodles, a symbol of longevity, never seem to end. Noodles play an important part in Asian cuisine. When I was in Singapore a few years ago, I was entranced by the melting pot represented by the colorful street food vendors. Here one could sample Chinese, Indian, Malaysian, and Eurasian delicacies within a few blocks. I found the combination of noodles and peanuts especially delicious, and have tried to create a "street food" salad from my memory. This noodle dish can be eaten hot or cold. You may vary the meat garnish by using pork or turkey, or omit it entirely for a vegetarian dish.

NOTE *The large holes on a box-type grater will shred the cucumber nicely.*

SERVES 4 TO 6

- 4 ounces Asian rice noodles *(see page 10)*
- 1 tablespoon sesame oil
- 2 cups cooked, shredded chicken breast
- 1 red bell pepper, seeded, deribbed, and diced
- 1 English cucumber, peeled and shredded *(see Note)*
- ½ cup thinly sliced green onions, including tender green tops
- ⅓ cup sesame seeds, toasted *(see page 21)*

DRESSING

- ½ cup peanut butter, smooth or crunchy
- 2 tablespoons honey
- 3 tablespoons tamari
- 2 tablespoons sesame oil
- 2 tablespoons chicken broth
- ¼ teaspoon red pepper flakes

PREPARATION

Break the noodles in half and cook according to the directions on the package. Do not overcook. Drain in a colander and rinse briefly under cold water. Shake the colander gently to drain completely. Toss with the 1 tablespoon sesame oil and set aside.

To make the dressing, in a small bowl, whisk together the peanut butter, honey, tamari, the 2 tablespoons sesame oil, the chicken broth, and red pepper flakes. (This may also be done in a food processor or a blender.) The dressing should have the consistency of syrup.

Place the noodles on a large platter and pour two-thirds of the dressing over them. Toss gently but thoroughly. When the noodles are coated with the dressing, arrange the chicken, bell pepper, cucumber, and green onions on top of the noodles. Sprinkle the sesame seeds on top of the salad. Pour the remaining dressing over all.

Serve at once, or cover tightly (so that the chicken does not dry out) and refrigerate for up to 24 hours.

CHAPTER 5 : seafood pasta salad

Music Festival Lobster Pasta Salad

The hills of New Hampshire are truly alive with the sound of music for six glorious weeks each summer. The New Hampshire Music Festival holds world-class concerts with a different superb soloist each week. Many local people as well as the summer folk are involved on a volunteer basis. The concerts are generally sold out; part of the enjoyment of going is seeing old friends and making new ones. Tailgate or picnic suppers before the evening's entertainment are common, and a pleasant way to start a festive evening. I enjoy serving this salad for such an occasion, rounding out the meal with slices of juicy ripe tomatoes, crusty rolls, and a crisp white wine. It, like the concerts, gets rave reviews! Homemade mayonnaise is a plus in this recipe. (See photograph, page 68.)

NOTE *You will need two 1¼-pound lobsters to produce 2 cups of lobster meat. It is easier to cut the lobster meat into chunks with sharp kitchen shears than with a knife. Lobster meat can also be found frozen in 12-ounce cans in the freezer section of the supermarket. Twelve ounces of frozen lobster will yield about 1½ cups.*

SERVES 4 TO 6

- 6 ounces orecchiette or small shells
- 2 cups cooked lobster meat, cut into bite-sized chunks *(see Note)*
- 1 cup diced celery
- ½ cup thinly sliced green onions, including tender green tops
- 2 tablespoons chopped fresh tarragon or 2 teaspoons dried tarragon, crumbled

DRESSING

- ¾ cup mayonnaise, homemade, *(page 19)* or high-quality purchased
- Salt and freshly ground black pepper
- 1 tablespoon tarragon vinegar

PREPARATION

Cook the pasta according to the directions on the package for al dente. Drain in a colander and rinse briefly under cold running water. Shake the colander gently to drain completely. Set aside.

To make the dressing, in a small bowl, whisk together the mayonnaise and salt and pepper to taste. Whisk in the vinegar.

Place the pasta in a large bowl and add the lobster, celery, green onions, and tarragon. Toss together gently. Pour the dressing over the mixture and toss again, gently but thoroughly. Cover and refrigerate for at least 1 hour and up to 8 hours. If you refrigerate the salad for 8 hours or more, you may want to add a small amount of mayonnaise, as the pasta will absorb the dressing over a long period of time. Serve chilled.

Udon and Shrimp Salad

Japanese udon noodles have a delicious mild, nutty flavor, and are made from either wheat or corn flour. They are frequently used in miso soup, as well as an addition to salads and vegetables. A rich golden color with either a square or a round shape, they are a perfect background for the delicate pink shrimp in this salad.

SERVES 6

○ 1 pound large shrimp *(16 to 20)*, shelled and deveined
○ 3 tablespoons peanut oil
○ 2 cloves garlic, minced
○ 2 teaspoons peeled, grated fresh ginger
○ 1 tablespoon rice wine vinegar
○ 8 ounces udon noodles
○ ½ English cucumber, peeled, seeded and cut into ¼ -inch dice
○ 3 green onions, including tender green tops, thinly sliced
○ ½ cup chopped cashews for garnish *(optional)*

DRESSING

○ 2 cloves garlic, minced
○ 2 tablespoons fresh lemon juice
○ 2 tablespoons rice wine vinegar
○ 2 tablespoons Asian fish sauce
○ 1 tablespoon sugar
○ ¼ teaspoon freshly ground black pepper
○ ½ cup peanut oil

PREPARATION

Combine the shrimp, 2 tablespoons of the peanut oil, the garlic, ginger, and the vinegar in a sealable plastic bag. Marinate in the refrigerator for 1 hour.

Cook the noodles according to the directions on the package. Do not overcook. Drain the noodles in a colander and rinse briefly under cold running water. Shake the colander gently to drain completely. Set aside.

Drain the shrimp and discard the marinade. Warm the remaining 1 tablespoon peanut oil in a skillet over medium-high heat. Add the marinated shrimp and sauté, stirring frequently, just until opaque throughout, about 4 minutes. Transfer to a bowl and set aside.

To make the dressing, in a small bowl, combine the garlic, lemon juice, the vinegar, the fish sauce, sugar, and pepper and whisk until the sugar is dissolved. Slowly whisk in the ½ cup peanut oil until an emulsion forms.

Place the noodles in a large bowl and add the shrimp, cucumber, and green onions. Pour the dressing over the mixture and toss gently but thoroughly. Serve at once, or cover and refrigerate for up to 8 hours. Garnish with the cashews just before serving, if desired.

Pasta Salad Niçoise

In French cuisine, this is known as a *salade composée* or "compound salad" — that is, a collection of several compatible foods. A classic niçoise salad is made with potatoes, but here a delicious variation on the traditional theme uses pasta instead of potatoes. Only the freshest and ripest of companion vegetables will do: juicy ripe tomatoes, crisp green beans, along with plump black olives. I serve this salad when I know we're in for a hot spell, because all the components can be made in the cool of morning and assembled just before serving. Arrange this salad on your prettiest platter.

SERVES 4 TO 6

- 6 ounces farfalle
- 4 ounces young green beans, trimmed, blanched *(see page 20)*, and cut into 1-inch pieces
- 2 ripe tomatoes, cut into quarters
- 3 hard-boiled eggs, quartered lengthwise
- 1 can *(6 ounces)* solid white-meat tuna in olive oil, drained and flaked
- 6 to 8 anchovy fillets in olive oil, rinsed and patted dry on paper towels
- ½ cup niçoise olives, pitted *(see page 15)*
- 2 tablespoons capers, drained

DRESSING

- Basic Vinaigrette *(page 18)*, doubled

PREPARATION

Cook the farfalle according to the directions on the package for al dente. Drain in a colander and rinse briefly under cold running water. Shake the colander gently to drain completely. Set aside.

Assemble the salad just before serving: On the serving platter, arrange the pasta, green beans, tomato wedges, egg quarters, and flaked tuna in an attractive pattern. Lay the anchovy fillets in a crisscross pattern across the top of the salad and sprinkle with the olives and capers. Drizzle enough vinaigrette over the salad to coat all the parts; you may not need the whole cup. Serve immediately.

You may assemble the salad up to 6 hours ahead. Cover and refrigerate. Add the dressing just before serving.

Boca Raton Asian Seafood Pasta Salad

Chef Louis Ellenbogen of the Boca Raton Resort in Boca Raton, Florida, is the creator of one of the best salads I have ever had the good fortune to eat. Chef Louis serves the salad at Nick's Fish Market, one of several excellent restaurants in the resort complex. He was kind enough to share the recipe with me on a recent visit to this tropical paradise. The salad is a tower of zesty flavor, loaded with crunch and emboldened with a combination of spicy and sweet flavors in each forkful. Although excellent mango salsa is becoming increasingly available in supermarkets, I've included a recipe for making your own, if you prefer or you can't locate a bottled variety. You could also substitute a good quality commercial peach or pineapple salsa.

NOTE *It's easy to make a fresh, flavorful mango salsa. In a bowl, combine 1 cup diced ripe mango, 1 teaspoon minced seeded jalapeño, 3 tablespoons coarsely chopped fresh cilantro, 2 tablespoons fresh lime juice, ¼ teaspoon salt, ⅛ teaspoon freshly ground black pepper and ⅓ cup minced red onion. Toss to mix thoroughly. Makes 1 cup.*

SERVES 4

- 8 ounces udon or soba noodles
- 1 cup shredded carrots
- 1 cup shredded red cabbage
- 1 cup shredded napa cabbage
- ½ cup mango salsa (see Note)
- 8 ounces lump crabmeat, flaked and any bits of shell or cartilage removed
- 4 large shrimp, cooked and deveined (optional)
- Fresh chive stalks and sesame seeds, toasted (see page 21), for garnish

DRESSING

- 3 tablespoons pickled ginger juice
- 6 tablespoons peanut oil
- 1 tablespoon sesame oil
- 2 tablespoons soy sauce
- ¼ cup sweet Thai chile sauce
- 2 teaspoons Chinese chile sauce
- 1 tablespoon chopped garlic
- 2 tablespoons pickled ginger, chopped

PREPARATION

Cook the noodles according to the directions on the package. Do not overcook. Drain in a colander and rinse briefly under cold running water. Shake the colander gently to drain completely. Set aside.

To make the dressing, in a small bowl, whisk together the pickled ginger juice, peanut oil, sesame oil, soy sauce, Thai and Chinese chile sauces, and garlic. Stir in the pickled ginger.

Place the noodles in a large serving bowl and add the carrot, cabbages, and mango salsa. Toss together gently. Add the crabmeat and toss gently again.

Pour the dressing over the mixture and toss one more time, gently but thoroughly.

Pile the mixture vertically on four individual salad plates or arrange on a large flat platter. If using shrimp, split each in two, leaving them attached at the head, and arrange fanned out on each plate or the platter. Garnish each serving with the chive stalks and sesame seeds and serve immediately, or cover and refrigerate for up to 6 hours.

Pipette and Surimi "Louis" Salad

Crab Louis is a classic seafood salad, found on many menus in better restaurants years ago. Depending on your source, it originated either in San Francisco, Seattle, or, as James Beard claims, in his hometown of Portland, Oregon. No one is quite sure who Louis was, but his creation is a tasty one. I've created my own version using surimi, a processed fish product found in most supermarkets in the freezer section, usually labeled "imitation crabmeat" or "imitation lobster." It is generally made from Alaskan pollack, by means of a process invented by the Japanese centuries ago. Surimi (which means minced or formed fish in Japanese) is widely used today in salad recipes calling for shellfish. Blended with other ingredients, you'd be hard pressed to tell the difference, although the taste is slightly sweeter.

SERVES 6 TO 8

- 8 ounces pipette or other small tubular pasta
- 12 ounces surimi, thawed according to package directions and shredded *(see recipe introduction)*
- Red-leaf lettuce leaves for serving
- 3 hard-boiled eggs, quartered
- ½ cup black olives, pitted *(see page 15)*

DRESSING

- 1 cup mayonnaise, homemade *(page 19)* or high-quality purchased
- ¼ cup heavy cream
- ⅓ cup chile sauce
- 2 teaspoons fresh lemon juice
- 1 teaspoon Worcestershire sauce
- Salt and freshly ground black pepper
- 3 tablespoons chopped green bell pepper
- 3 tablespoons chopped green onions, including tender green tops

PREPARATION

Cook the pasta according to the directions on the package for al dente. Drain in a colander and rinse briefly under cold running water. Shake the colander gently to drain completely. Set aside.

To make the dressing, in a bowl, whisk together the mayonnaise, cream, chile sauce, lemon juice, Worcestershire sauce, and salt and pepper to taste. Stir in the bell pepper and green onions.

Place the pasta in a large serving bowl and add the surimi. Toss together gently. Pour the dressing over the mixture and toss again, gently but thoroughly. Line a large platter with the lettuce leaves and place the pasta mixture on them. Arrange the egg sections and olives on top in an attractive pattern and serve at once, or cover and refrigerate for up to 8 hours.

Heartland Mussels and Shells Salad

Growing up on the coast of New England, I was always fortunate enough to have the freshest seafood available. It was only when I moved to the Midwest that I realized the rest of the world did not necessarily enjoy or even appreciate this luxury. When the new specialty seafood counter opened in a corner of our local supermarket in Ohio, I was delighted. One Monday I saw some fresh, shiny mussels displayed in the case. I immediately thought of the class I was teaching later in the week and decided to change my lesson plan. "Mmm, those look nice, will you have mussels on Thursday?" I inquired. With a perfectly straight face the young girl behind the counter replied, "If I don't sell them, I will." Things have improved. Nowadays you can certainly find the ingredients for this tasty salad easily in the heartland and elsewhere.

SERVES 6

- 8 ounces small shells
- 2 pounds mussels
- 1 cup dry white wine
- ½ cup chopped shallots
- 1 fresh thyme sprig or 1 teaspoon dried thyme, crumbled
- 5 fresh curly parsley sprigs, plus ¼ cup chopped parsley for garnish
- 1 teaspoon freshly ground black pepper
- 2 tablespoons chopped fresh chives for garnish

DRESSING

- ¼ cup white wine vinegar
- 1 tablespoon whole-grain Dijon mustard
- 1 tablespoon dry white wine
- Salt and freshly ground black pepper
- ½ cup extra-virgin olive oil
- 1 tablespoon capers, drained and chopped

PREPARATION

Cook the shells according to the directions on the package for al dente. Drain in a colander and rinse briefly under cold running water. Shake the colander gently to drain completely, making sure no water is trapped in the shells. Set aside.

To prepare the mussels, scrub them with a stiff brush to remove any sand or grit, and remove any protruding beards (the dark, spongy matter that is sometimes found in the seam where the shells meet). Discard any mussels that are cracked or do not close to the touch. Put the mussels, the wine, shallots, thyme, and parsley sprigs in a large pot. Bring to a rapid boil over high heat and cook until the mussels open, about 5 to 7 minutes. Lift the mussels out of the pot with a slotted spoon, discarding any that have not opened. Remove the mussel meats from the shells and place in a bowl.

To make the dressing, in a small bowl whisk together the vinegar, mustard, the wine, and salt and pepper to taste. Add the olive oil gradually, whisking until an emulsion forms. Stir in the capers.

Combine the pasta shells and the mussel meats in a large bowl and pour the dressing over the mixture. Toss gently but thoroughly. Garnish with the chopped parsley, black pepper, and chives and serve at once, or cover and refrigerate for up to 6 hours.

Manicotti Stuffed with Tuna Salad

I love stuffed pasta, in any form. Cannelloni, manicotti, lasagna, I'll eat it all! But why must these delicious combinations be limited to hot dishes? Finding a can of Italian tuna and some manicotti tubes in my cupboard one day, I made this stuffed pasta, to be served chilled, for an impromptu lunch. A tossed green salad or a platter of ruby red tomato slices round out the meal. This salad makes a delicious addition to a summer buffet, and can easily be doubled.

SERVES 6

- 9 manicotti shells
- 2 cans *(6 ounces each)* tuna, preferably oil-packed Italian, drained, 2 tablespoons oil reserved
- ½ cup finely chopped celery
- 2 tablespoons capers, drained and chopped, plus extra for garnish
- ¼ cup minced red onion
- Red lettuce leaves for serving
- 2 red bell peppers, roasted *(see page 20)* and cut into strips, for garnish

DRESSING

- ¾ cup mayonnaise, homemade *(page 19)* or high-quality purchased, plus ½ cup additional mayonnaise for garnish
- 1 tablespoon white balsamic vinegar
- ½ teaspoon salt
- ¼ teaspoon freshly ground black pepper
- 1 clove garlic, minced

PREPARATION

Cook the manicotti according to the directions on the package for al dente. Drain in a colander and rinse briefly under cold running water. Shake the colander gently and then transfer the manicotti tubes to paper towels to drain completely. Cut each piece in half; a diagonal cut is attractive. Set aside.

Place the tuna in a bowl, flake gently, and add the celery, chopped capers, and onion. Toss together gently and set aside.

To make the dressing, in a small bowl, whisk together the ¾ cup mayonnaise, the vinegar, salt, pepper, and garlic. Whisk in the reserved tuna oil. Pour the dressing over the tuna mixture and toss together gently but thoroughly.

Using a long-handled spoon such as an ice-tea spoon, carefully stuff the manicotti pieces with the tuna mixture, working from both ends, until they are filled but not packed so much that they split. You may refrigerate them, covered, for up to 8 hours at this point. When ready to serve, arrange three pieces on each of 6 individual plates, or arrange on a large platter lined with the lettuce leaves. Garnish each manicotti with a dollop of the additional mayonnaise and arrange the roasted pepper strips and whole capers on top of the mayonnaise.

Salmon, Peas, and Pasta Salad with Dill Dressing

The Fourth of July is a special day in New England. We celebrate with parades, fireworks, and of course delicious summer food. In my town of Center Harbor, New Hampshire, the day begins with a footrace starting from the fire station. The parade follows, featuring a local high school band or sometimes the Mad Bavarians, a German-style band of note. Since my house affords a good view of the lake, I invite friends for supper on the porch. The fireworks begin at dusk, and the sky is illuminated with the brilliant display, arching out over the lake. Boats come from all around to observe the display from the water, their lights appearing like an armada of fireflies. Here is a recipe I serve on this festive occasion, salmon and peas being traditional New England Fourth-of-July fare.

SERVES 8

- 6 ounces mini-penne or other small pasta
- 1 pound salmon steaks or fillets, poached or grilled, then skinned and flaked
- 1½ cups fresh peas, blanched *(see page 20)*, or frozen baby peas, thawed
- ¼ cup finely chopped red onion
- 1 tomato, peeled *(see page 20)*, seeded *(see page 15)*, and diced

DRESSING

- 2 tablespoons white wine vinegar
- 2 tablespoons fresh lemon juice
- 1 tablespoon sugar
- ½ teaspoon salt
- 2 tablespoons whole-grain Dijon mustard
- ⅓ cup extra-virgin olive oil
- ¼ cup finely chopped fresh dill

PREPARATION

Cook the pasta according to the directions on the package for al dente. Drain in a colander and rinse briefly under cold running water. Shake the colander gently to drain completely. Set aside.

To make the dressing, in a small bowl, whisk together the vinegar, lemon juice, sugar, salt, and mustard. Add the olive oil gradually, whisking until an emulsion forms. Whisk in the dill.

Place the salmon, peas, onion, and tomato in a large serving bowl. (If you are refrigerating the salad, do not add the peas until just before serving, as the acid in the dressing will cause them to discolor.) Add the pasta and toss together gently. Pour the dressing over the mixture and toss again, gently but thoroughly. Serve immediately, or cover and refrigerate for up to 8 hours.

Campanelle, Artichoke, and Anchovy Salad

I included anchovies in the title of this salad so you will know right away if you wish to continue reading. People are strongly opinionated about anchovies: They either like them, or they don't. There is no middle ground. The little "furry fish," as my children used to call them, are essential to a good Caesar salad in my mind, but I've ordered it in restaurants only to be asked, "Hold the anchovies?" In my cooking classes I use anchovy paste in many recipes; it lends a subtle layer of flavor that most people can't discern (a little-known fact is that it is an important ingredient in Worcestershire sauce). If you are an anchovy fan and have had the opportunity to taste the Italian anchovies that come packed in salt, you know just how good they can be.

SERVES 6

- 8 ounces campanelle
- 1 package *(9 ounces)* frozen artichoke hearts, cooked, drained, and quartered
- 4 Roma *(plum)* tomatoes, peeled *(see page 20)*, seeded *(see page 15)*, and chopped
- ¼ cup chopped fresh flat-leaf parsley
- ½ cup kalamata olives, pitted *(see page 15)* and chopped
- 8 anchovy fillets, rinsed, patted dry on paper towels, and chopped
- 1 tablespoon capers, drained, for garnish

DRESSING

- Juice of 1 lemon
- 1 clove garlic, minced
- 1 teaspoon anchovy paste
- Salt and freshly ground black pepper
- ½ cup extra-virgin olive oil

PREPARATION

Cook the campanelle according to the directions on the package for al dente. Drain in a colander and rinse briefly under cold running water. Shake the colander gently to drain completely. Set aside.

To make the dressing, in a small bowl, whisk together the lemon juice, garlic, anchovy paste, and salt and pepper to taste. Add the olive oil gradually, whisking until an emulsion forms.

Place the pasta in a large serving bowl. Add the artichoke hearts, tomatoes, parsley, olives, and anchovies. Toss together gently. Pour the dressing over the mixture and toss again, gently but thoroughly. Sprinkle the capers over the salad. Serve immediately, or cover and refrigerate for up to 8 hours. Bring the salad to room temperature before serving.

Crabmeat Salad Shells

Robby Graham of Warren, Maine, sells the best seafood imaginable. His refrigerated truck is found every Friday at the base of High School Hill on Route 25 in Meredith, New Hampshire. His sweet and delicious crabmeat is that of the Pikki Toe crab, which is smaller than the rock or Jonah crab. It is hand-picked to remove cartilage and shell. Robby tells me the handpicking process, historically done by the fisherman's wife, is a real talent, much more labor intensive than machine picking. The machine-picked crab is flooded with water to float the shells, then compressed to remove the water, losing some flavor in the process. The choicest parts of the crab are the legs, but the body meat is sweet and luscious as well.

SERVES 6

- 20 large pasta shells
- 1 pound lump crabmeat
- 2 red bell peppers, roasted *(see page 20)* and cut in thin strips
- Lettuce leaves for serving
- ¼ cup finely chopped fresh flat-leaf parsley for garnish

DRESSING

- ¾ cup mayonnaise, homemade *(page 19)* or high-quality purchased
- 2 tablespoons capers, drained
- ½ teaspoon dry mustard
- 2 tablespoons minced shallot
- 1 tablespoon minced fresh flat-leaf parsley
- Dash of red hot sauce, or to taste

PREPARATION

Cook the shells according to the directions on the package for al dente. Drain them in a colander and rinse briefly under cold running water. Shake the colander gently, then transfer the shells, open side down, to paper towels to drain completely.

Put the crabmeat in a bowl and flake it, discarding any bits of shell and cartilage.

To make the dressing, stir together the mayonnaise, capers, mustard, shallot, minced parsley, and hot sauce. Pour the dressing over the flaked crabmeat and toss gently but thoroughly.

Using a teaspoon, stuff each shell with some of the crabmeat mixture. Place one roasted pepper strip lengthwise across each shell opening. Arrange the lettuce on a large platter, and arrange the filled shells over them. Cover and refrigerate for at least 1 hour and up to 8 hours. Sprinkle with the chopped parsley just before serving.

CHAPTER 6 : from family and friends

Ellen's Couscous, Lentil, and Pasta Salad

Ellen Ogden, a talented cookbook author, gardener, and mother, shared this recipe with me to adapt for pasta when I told her I was writing this book. We discovered, after being introduced by a mutual friend, that we had much in common. We are both northern New Englanders, members of the International Association of Culinary Professionals, and both derive much pleasure from writing about food. She was cofounder of the *The Cook's Garden* seed catalogue, recognized as the ultimate source for European-style salad greens and heirloom vegetables, flowers, and herbs. Her first book, *The Cook's Garden,* is a treasure trove of information. This salad, bursting with nutrition as well as flavor, will serve a large group, and benefits from being made ahead.

NOTE *If you are making this salad more than 2 hours ahead of serving, you may want to increase the amount of dressing by one half and reserve a little to toss with the salad just before serving, as couscous tends to absorb dressing quickly.*

SERVES 10 TO 12

6 ounces ditalini or other small pasta
1 cup green or brown lentils
1 package *(10 ounces)* plain couscous
2 cups grape or cherry tomatoes, halved
6 green onions, including tender green tops, coarsely chopped
½ cup pine nuts, toasted *(see page 21)*
2 cups mesclun, coarsely chopped
1 cup crumbled feta cheese for garnish

DRESSING *(see Note)*

3 tablespoons red wine vinegar
¼ cup fresh lemon juice
2 cloves garlic, minced
Salt and freshly ground black pepper
½ cup extra-virgin olive oil

PREPARATION

Cook the pasta according to the directions on the package for al dente. Drain in a colander and rinse briefly under cold running water. Shake the colander gently to drain completely. Set aside.

While the pasta is cooking, place the lentils in a saucepan with cold water to cover by two inches. Bring to a boil, reduce the heat, and simmer just until tender, about 15 minutes. Drain well and transfer to a large serving bowl to cool.

Cook the couscous according the directions on the package. Fluff the couscous with a fork and add it to the lentils. Add the pasta to the couscous mixture.

To make the dressing, place the vinegar and lemon juice in a small bowl. Whisk in the garlic and salt and pepper to taste. Gradually whisk in the olive oil until an emulsion forms.

Add the tomatoes, green onions, and pine nuts to the couscous mixture. Toss together gently. Add the dressing and toss again, gently but thoroughly. Cover and refrigerate for at least 2 hours and up to 6 hours before serving. Just before serving, toss in the mesclun and sprinkle with the feta.

The Roommate's Vermicelli Salad

My freshman-year roommate at Smith College in Northampton, Massachusetts, was a young lady by the name of Ann Alspaugh. We had not chosen each other—it was luck of the draw—and were truly two girls from the opposite ends of the earth, as far as we were concerned. The first few days we had trouble understanding each other's accents, she from Duncan, Oklahoma, and I from Hingham, Massachusetts. We soon became fast friends, though, and are to this day. Ann returned to Oklahoma, and is known throughout the state and country as a patron of the arts and benefactress of innumerable good causes, not the least of which are the concerns of Native Americans and preserving the art of the West. She is the consummate hostess, and has given me her recipe for a delicious pasta salad. She advises breaking the vermicelli before cooking it—it's easier to eat that way, particularly in a buffet situation. The pasta marinates overnight, so this is an excellent do-ahead recipe.

SERVES 8

- 1 pound vermicelli
- 1 cup safflower oil
- ½ cup fresh lemon juice
- 1 tablespoon Accent seasoning *(optional)*
- ½ cup thinly sliced celery
- 1 can *(8 ounces)* sliced water chestnuts, drained
- ½ red bell pepper, seeded, deribbed, and diced
- ½ cup chopped red onion
- 2 tablespoons capers, drained
- ⅓ cup freshly grated Parmesan cheese for garnish

DRESSING

- ½ cup mayonnaise, homemade *(page 19)* or high-quality purchased
- 1 tablespoon white wine vinegar
- Salt and freshly ground black pepper

PREPARATION

Break the vermicelli in half and cook according to the directions on the package for al dente. Drain in a colander and rinse briefly under cold running water. Shake the colander gently to drain completely. Place the pasta in a large serving bowl.

Whisk together the oil, lemon juice, and Accent in a small bowl. Toss with the pasta, cover, and refrigerate overnight.

The next day, add the celery, water chestnuts, bell pepper, onion, and capers to the pasta. Toss together gently.

To make the dressing, in a small bowl whisk together the mayonnaise, vinegar, and salt and pepper to taste.

Fold the dressing into the salad and toss gently but thoroughly. Sprinkle the Parmesan over the salad. Serve immediately, or cover and refrigerate for up to 8 hours.

Kathryn's Gemelli Salad with Sun-Dried Tomatoes and Artichokes

Kathryn Ellis Moore of Groton, Massachusetts, believes potlucks are the ideal way to entertain for today's multi-tasking cooks. She enjoys the sense of communality that is evoked when everyone contributes and the added advantage that it makes for far less work for all involved. Kathryn is the busy mother of two young boys, Michael and Gabriel, and has to budget her time. She advises prospective potluckers to bring their own serving implements and be willing to take the dish home dirty! A talented cook, she contributed this recipe to an article about potlucks in the *Boston Globe*. She graciously agreed to share it with me. Kathryn notes that in the summer she adds fresh oregano and thyme from her garden.

SERVES 8 OR MORE

- 1 pound gemelli
- 2 tablespoons olive oil
- 1 large red onion, finely chopped
- 2 cloves garlic, finely chopped
- ¾ cup oil-packed sun-dried tomatoes, drained with oil reserved, cut into julienne
- 1 cup oil-packed artichoke hearts, drained with oil reserved, quartered
- 2 tablespoons capers, drained
- 1 tablespoon balsamic vinegar
- ½ teaspoon brown sugar
- Pinch of cayenne pepper
- Salt and freshly ground black pepper
- ⅓ cup loosely packed fresh basil leaves, cut into chiffonade *(see page 15)*
- Flowering ends of basil sprigs for garnish *(optional)*
- ½ cup crumbled feta cheese *(optional)*

PREPARATION

Cook the gemelli according to the directions on the package for al dente. Drain in a colander and rinse briefly under cold running water. Shake the colander again gently to drain completely.

While the pasta is cooking, heat the olive oil in a skillet over medium heat. Add the onion and cook, stirring often, until it softens, about 5 minutes. Add the garlic and cook for 1 minute longer, being careful not to let it burn. Add the sun-dried tomatoes and artichokes with their oils, the capers, vinegar, brown sugar, and cayenne. Season with salt and pepper to taste. Remove the pan from the heat and add the sliced basil.

Place the pasta in a large serving bowl and add the sun-dried tomato mixture. Toss together gently. Garnish with flowering basil sprigs and sprinkle with feta, if desired. Serve warm or at room temperature, or cover and refrigerate for up to 6 hours. Return to room temperature before serving.

Wendy's Rotini and Smoked Salmon Salad with Tomato-Basil Vinaigrette

Wendy Van de Poll is a very special person. A massage therapist whose clients include "Humans, Horses, and Hounds," she practices her skills in Center Sandwich, New Hampshire, in a charming rural setting. I can't speak for the canines and equines, but a visit to Wendy's takes care of any of my computer-related aches and pains. While working her magic one day, she told me about this delicious salad she makes for her husband, Rick.

NOTE *If you prefer, ¾ cup homemade (page 19) or high-quality purchased mayonnaise, may be substituted for the vinaigrette. Wendy sprinkles the mayonnaise version with ½ cup crumbled feta cheese.*

SERVES 6

- 6 to 8 ounces tricolor rotini
- 4 ounces smoked salmon fillet, crumbled
- ½ cup kalamata olives, pitted *(see page 15)* and chopped
- 2 tablespoons capers, drained
- ½ red bell pepper, seeded, deribbed, and finely diced
- ½ cup oil-packed artichoke hearts, drained and chopped
- ½ cup frozen baby peas, thawed
- ½ cup frozen corn kernels, thawed
- 4 tablespoons unsalted sunflower seeds, toasted *(see page 21)*

DRESSING *(see Note)*

- 3 tablespoons rice wine vinegar
- ¼ cup oil-packed sun-dried tomatoes, drained and finely chopped
- Salt and freshly ground black pepper
- ½ cup extra-virgin olive oil
- ¼ cup finely chopped fresh basil

PREPARATION

Cook the rotini according to the directions on the package for al dente. Drain in a colander and rinse briefly under cold running water. Shake the colander gently to drain completely. Set aside.

To make the dressing, in small bowl, whisk together the vinegar, sun-dried tomatoes, and salt and pepper to taste. Gradually whisk in the olive oil until an emulsion forms. Stir the basil.

Place the pasta in a large salad bowl and add the salmon, olives, capers, bell pepper, artichokes hearts, peas, and corn. Toss together gently. Pour the vinaigrette over the mixture and toss again, gently but thoroughly. Sprinkle the sunflower seeds and feta cheese, if using, over the salad. Cover and refrigerate for up to 2 hours before serving. Serve chilled.

Lisa's Exploding Asian Noodle Salad

My daughter, Lisa, offered this recipe as her contribution to this collection. Not only has she received her doctorate in history from Harvard, she is also an amazing cook. However, when first married, she prepared this dish for husband Bill with lasting repercussions. It seems, while preparing the dressing, she did not replace the lid on the pot quickly enough. The seeds exploded all over the kitchen, coating the ceiling, walls, and stove vent with a patina of sesame seeds. When they moved out of the apartment at the end of their lease, the landlord added an extra cleaning charge to remove the sticky reminder of what she still says is a good dish. Moral of the story: Be fast with the lid!

NOTE *Asian rice sticks may also be called vermicelli, or angel hair. Vermicelli or cappellini (angel hair pasta) may be substituted.*

SERVES 4

- 8 ounces Asian rice noodles *(see page 10)*
- 6 green onions, including tender green tops, chopped
- ¼ cup pine nuts, toasted *(see page 21)*
- 1½ cups chopped cooked shrimp *(optional)*
- Romaine leaves for garnish

DRESSING

- ¾ cup peanut oil
- 1 tablespoon sesame oil
- 1 tablespoon sesame seeds
- 1½ tablespoons ground coriander
- ⅓ cup soy sauce
- 1 teaspoon hot chile oil, or to taste

PREPARATION

Cook the noodles according to the directions on the package. Do not overcook. Drain in a colander and rinse briefly under cold running water. Shake the colander gently to drain completely. Set aside.

To make the dressing, place the peanut and sesame oils and the sesame seeds in a small saucepan over medium heat. Cook just until the sesame seeds begin to turn golden brown, 3 or 4 minutes. Remove from the heat and stir in the coriander and soy sauce, covering the pan immediately as the mixture begins to sputter and sizzle. When the sizzle has subsided, remove the lid and stir in the chile oil.

Place the noodles in a large serving bowl and add the green onions, pine nuts, and shrimp, if using. Toss together gently. Pour the dressing over the mixture and toss again, gently but thoroughly. Cover and refrigerate for at least 3 hours and up to 24 hours. Serve on a large platter lined with the lettuce leaves.

Helen's Farfalle Salad with Lemon-Caper Dressing

My friend Helen Heiner is a transplanted Californian. She started taking my cooking classes when she moved to New Hampshire from San Francisco many years ago, and we became fast friends. Along with being a busy RN in a local doctor's office, she is an excellent cook in her own right. We've had many adventures in the kitchen together preparing food for local events, such as an opening at the League of New Hampshire Craftsmen Store or a political tea for candidates stumping through the state. Helen contributed this salad from what she calls her "California repertoire."

SERVES 6

- 8 ounces farfalle
- ½ cup kalamata olives, pitted *(see page 15)* and chopped
- ½ cup frozen baby peas, thawed
- 1 red onion, halved vertically and thinly sliced
- 1 red bell pepper, seeded, deribbed, and chopped
- ¼ chopped fresh flat-leaf parsley

DRESSING

- 3 tablespoons red wine vinegar
- ½ teaspoon grated lemon zest
- 1 tablespoon fresh lemon juice
- 1 tablespoon capers, drained, plus 1 tablespoon caper liquid
- 2 cloves garlic, minced
- 2 teaspoons Dijon whole-grain mustard
- ½ teaspoon dried oregano, crumbled
- ½ teaspoon salt
- ⅛ teaspoon freshly ground black pepper
- ⅔ cup extra-virgin olive oil

PREPARATION

Cook the farfalle according to the directions on the package for al dente. Drain in a colander and rinse briefly under cold running water. Shake the colander gently to drain completely. Set aside.

To make the dressing, in a small bowl, whisk together the vinegar, lemon zest and juice, the liquid from the capers, the garlic, mustard, oregano, salt, and pepper. Gradually whisk in the olive oil until an emulsion forms. Stir in the capers.

Place the pasta, olives, peas, onion, bell pepper, and parsley in a large serving bowl. Toss together gently. Pour the dressing over the mixture and toss again, gently but thoroughly. Cover and refrigerate for at least 1 hour and up to 24 hours.

Alex and Andy's Rotini and Black Bean Salad

Mary Lee is the mother of twin boys, Alex and Andy, college students who enjoy their mother's cooking immensely and are the inspiration for her culinary endeavors. Mary takes my cooking classes and offered this recipe when I was discussing the pasta salad book project in class. When the boys were home in high school, Mary was famous for hosting team feeds. Since the boys were involved in tennis, cross country, soccer, and drama, as well as the math team and student council, Mary produced good food in quantity, thinking nothing of whipping up six jumbo pans of various pastas and homemade sauces, salads with homemade vinaigrette, and garlic bread. Her famous chocolate chip–oatmeal cookies sustained the cast and crew of the musical *L'il Abner* (Andy was Abner). The black beans and avocado are the boys' contribution to this delicious salad.

NOTE *The amount of vinegar can be adjusted. Mary's family likes the piquant flavor of more vinegar.*

SERVES 8

- 8 ounces rotini
- 1 can *(19 ounces)* black beans, drained and rinsed
- ½ cup grape or cherry tomatoes, halved
- ½ cup fresh corn kernels, blanched *(see page 20)*, or ½ cup frozen corn, thawed
- ¼ cup chopped green onions, white parts only
- ¼ cup chopped fresh chives or tender green tops of the onions *(above)*
- 2 tablespoons chopped fresh cilantro
- 1 ripe avocado for garnish
- Juice of ½ lemon

DRESSING

- ¼ to ½ cup balsamic vinegar *(see Note)*
- ½ teaspoon minced garlic
- Salt and freshly ground black pepper
- ¼ cup extra-virgin olive oil or grapeseed oil

PREPARATION

Cook the rotini according to the directions on the package for al dente. Drain in a colander and rinse briefly under cold running water. Shake the colander gently to drain completely. Set aside.

To make the dressing, in a small bowl, whisk together the vinegar, garlic, and salt and pepper to taste. Slowly whisk in the olive oil until an emulsion forms.

Place the drained pasta in a large serving bowl; add the beans, tomatoes, corn, green onions, chives, and cilantro. Toss together gently. Pour the dressing over the pasta mixture and toss again, gently but thoroughly. Cover and refrigerate for at least 1 hour and up to 24 hours. Just before serving, peel and dice the avocado and toss with the lemon juice. Sprinkle the avocado over the salad and serve.

Jo's Campanelle Salad with Tomatoes, Basil, and Brie

My sister, Jo, told me no collection of pasta salads would be complete without the all-time favorite of her reading group, which has been meeting for over twenty years. No one remembers how the recipe evolved, but it is served in late summer, when the local tomatoes are bursting with goodness and fresh basil is readily available. The choice of a meltingly ripe Brie cheese is key. The fanciful shape of the campanelle traps the lush juice of the tomatoes and creamy Brie. If food fuels the mind, the reading group is well energized by this luscious dish, truly the essence of summer.

NOTE *The cheese is easier to cut when it is cold. Remove some of the rind from the surface if you wish, by scraping across the cheese surface with a cheese plane.*

SERVES 6 TO 8

- 8 ounces campanelle

DRESSING

- 3 very ripe fresh tomatoes, peeled *(see page 20)*, seeded *(see page 15)*, and diced
- 1 cup loosely packed fresh basil leaves, cut into chiffonade *(see page 15)*
- 2 cloves garlic, minced
- 1 tablespoon balsamic vinegar
- Salt and freshly ground black pepper
- ½ cup extra-virgin olive oil
- 8 ounces ripe chilled Brie, some skin removed, cut into small chunks *(see Note)*

PREPARATION

Cook the campanelle according to the directions on the package for al dente. Drain in a colander and rinse briefly under cold running water. Shake the colander gently to drain completely. Set aside.

To make the dressing, place the tomatoes in a bowl. Add the basil, garlic, vinegar, and salt and pepper to taste. Toss to combine. Stir in the olive oil until well incorporated. Add the Brie to the tomato mixture and toss together gently.

Place the pasta in a large serving bowl. Pour the tomato mixture over and toss again, gently but thoroughly. Serve at once, or cover and refrigerate for up to 1 hour.

Beede Falls Orzo Salad

My close friend Maxiene Glenday is New Hampshire born and bred. She knows the state well. A favorite spot of hers in the summer months is the breathtakingly beautiful Beede Falls, a place of peace and tranquility not far from her home in Center Sandwich, New Hampshire. The Bear Camp River rushes over rocks and tumbles down, creating a wide waterfall that ends in a sparkling pool. It is too cold for swimming most of the summer, but the flat rocks that circle the beautiful pool of crystal-clear water are an ideal spot on which to spread a picnic. She has taken this salad of orzo and olives to the falls on several occasions. It can be made ahead and travels well.

SERVES 6

○ 8 ounces orzo
○ 1 cup cracked green olives, pitted *(see page 15)* and chopped
○ 1 cup oil-packed black olives, pitted *(see page 15)* and chopped
○ 4 green onions, including tender green tops, thinly sliced
○ ⅓ cup finely chopped fresh chives
○ 1 red bell pepper, roasted *(see page 20)* and diced
○ ½ cup pine nuts, toasted *(see page 21)*, for garnish

DRESSING

○ 3 tablespoons fresh lemon juice
○ 1 clove garlic, minced
○ Salt and freshly ground black pepper
○ ½ cup extra-virgin olive oil

PREPARATION

Cook the orzo according to the directions on the package for al dente. Drain in a colander and rinse briefly under cold running water. Shake the colander gently to drain completely. Set aside.

To make the dressing, in a small bowl, whisk together the lemon juice, garlic, and salt and pepper to taste. Gradually whisk in the olive oil until an emulsion forms.

Place the orzo in a large shallow bowl and add the green olives, black olives, green onions, chives and bell pepper. Toss together gently. Pour the dressing over the mixture and toss gently but thoroughly. Sprinkle the pine nuts over the salad and serve immediately, or cover and refrigerate for up to 24 hours.

Susan and Paolo's Yale Pasta Salad

While visiting their cousin Susan and her Italian husband, Paolo, a graduate student at Yale, my friends the Laphams were served this delicious pasta salad. Liz was amazed at how quickly Paolo threw it together, effortlessly producing a tasty meal. The mozzarella softens slightly when it comes in contact with the pasta. In Italy, this dish would be served as a separate course, but by simply adding some crusty bread and a glass of robust red wine, you certainly have a satisfying lunch or light dinner dish.

- 1 pound fusilli or rotini
- 8 ounces packaged or deli mozzarella cheese, cut into ½-inch cubes
- 2 cups cherry tomatoes, halved
- 3 green onions, including tender green tops, finely sliced
- ½ cup loosely packed fresh basil leaves, cut into chiffonade *(see page 15)*
- ¼ cup extra-virgin olive oil
- 1 tablespoon fresh lemon juice
- 1 teaspoon salt
- Freshly ground black pepper
- Freshly grated Parmesan cheese

PREPARATION

Cook the pasta according to directions on the package for al dente. Drain in a colander, shaking the colander to drain completely. Do not rinse the pasta.

Place the mozzarella, tomatoes, green onions, and basil in a large bowl and pour the warm pasta over the contents of the bowl. Pour the olive oil over all, sprinkle with the lemon juice, and toss gently. Season with the salt and black pepper to taste. Serve at room temperature.

Fold the dressing into the salad and toss gently but thoroughly. Sprinkle the Parmesan over the salad. Serve immediately, or cover and refrigerate for up to 8 hours.

Endeavor Café Pasta Salad

The Sandwich General Store and Endeavor Café is located at the classic New England crossroads featured at the opening of Bob Newhart's delightful innkeeper television series. When the general store that had been serving the residents of Center Sandwich, New Hampshire, closed down in 2001, a group of concerned citizens pooled their efforts and finances to reopen the store, and added a café serving breakfast and lunch. Had this not happened, people would have had to drive miles for a loaf of bread or a newspaper. Now, café breakfasts feature crisp waffles and feather-light pancakes, swimming in good New Hampshire maple syrup. At lunchtime, the café serves delicious homemade soups, hearty sandwiches, quiches, and salads. Tempting prepared dishes to take home are also available. Megan Dodge, one of the store's staff, graciously shared her pasta salad recipe with me. She told me the first time she made it, the staff ate it all and they had nothing left to sell. She uses only the freshest vegetables and herbs from the certified organic Booty Farm, in town.

SERVES 6 TO 8

- ½ cup extra-virgin olive oil
- ½ cup finely chopped fresh basil
- 1 clove garlic, chopped
- Salt and freshly ground black pepper
- 12 ounces tricolor rotini or any spiral shape
- 3 large tomatoes, seeded *(see page 15)* and diced
- ½ cup freshly grated Parmesan cheese

PREPARATION

In a small bowl, combine the olive oil, basil, garlic, and salt and pepper to taste. Let the mixture stand for the time it takes to cook the pasta.

Cook the pasta according to the directions on the package for al dente. Drain in a colander and rinse briefly under cold running water. Shake the colander gently to drain completely.

Place the pasta in a large serving bowl. Add the tomatoes and Parmesan and toss together gently. Pour the flavored oil over the mixture and toss again, gently but thoroughly. Serve immediately, or cover and refrigerate for up to 4 hours. If you wish to refrigerate the salad for a longer time, do not add the basil until serving time.

CH's Orzo Salad with Spinach, Olives, and Feta

My son, CH, and his wife, Lisa, are typical of many young marrieds today. They both have full-time jobs and yet manage to spend quality time with their adorable sons, Jake and Sam. Commuting to New York City and having different schedules doesn't allow much time for cooking during the week, but on the weekends they pull out all the stops. We call CH "the grillmeister" for his devotion to firing up the grill in all seasons. This luscious orzo salad is a favorite side dish they often serve with grilled lamb.

SERVES 4 TO 6

- 8 ounces orzo
- 4 cups fresh baby spinach leaves, stems removed, torn if large
- 2 celery stalks, chopped
- 1 cup kalamata olives, pitted *(see page 15)* and chopped
- ½ cup chopped red onion
- 4 ounces feta cheese, crumbled

DRESSING

- 2 tablespoons white wine vinegar
- Salt and freshly ground black pepper
- 1 teaspoon anchovy paste
- 1 large clove garlic clove, minced
- ⅓ cup extra-virgin olive oil

PREPARATION

Cook the orzo according to the directions on the package for al dente. Drain in a colander and rinse briefly under cold running water. Shake the colander gently to drain completely. Set aside.

To make the dressing, place the vinegar in a small bowl and whisk in salt and pepper to taste. Add the anchovy paste and garlic, then slowly whisk in the olive oil until an emulsion forms.

Place the orzo in a large serving bowl; add the spinach, celery, olives, onion, and feta, and toss together gently. Pour the dressing over the mixture and toss again, gently but thoroughly. Cover and refrigerate for up to 4 hours, or serve immediately.

Waterfall Café Pasta Salad

After my stalwart walking group finishes its Friday stride through the picturesque streets of Meredith, New Hampshire, we adjourn to the Waterfall Café, located in the Inn at Mill Falls. The café is situated overlooking the tumbling waterfall that cascades from Lake Waukewan to Lake Winnipesaukee. Its waters once powered a linen mill, now the site of attractive shops and lodging. The small café emanates warmth and welcome. As we tuck vigorously into the tender muffins, chewy bagels, and hot coffee, we assure ourselves that by our vigorous walk we have earned the treat. The owner, Suzanne Thompson, serves not only hearty New England breakfasts but tasty lunches as well. The chef, Patte Morrow, graciously shared their delicious pasta salad recipe with me.

SERVES 6 TO 8

- 8 ounces rotini or fusilli
- ⅓ cup oil-packed sun-dried tomatoes, drained with 1 tablespoon of oil reserved, chopped
- ½ red bell pepper, seeded, deribbed, and diced
- ½ green bell pepper, seeded, deribbed, and diced
- 1 cup chopped fresh spinach leaves
- 2 grated carrots, peeled and grated
- ½ cup loosely packed fresh basil leaves, cut into chiffonade *(see page 15)*
- ½ cup kalamata olives, pitted *(see page 15)* and chopped
- ½ cup crumbled feta cheese

DRESSING

- 3 tablespoons balsamic vinegar
- 1 clove garlic, minced
- Salt and freshly ground black pepper
- ½ cup extra-virgin olive oil

PREPARATION

Cook the pasta according to the directions on the package for al dente. Drain in a colander and rinse briefly under cold running water. Shake the colander gently to drain completely. Toss with the reserved tomato oil and set aside.

To make the dressing, in a small bowl, whisk together the vinegar, garlic, and salt and pepper to taste. Gradually add the olive oil, whisking until an emulsion forms.

Place the pasta in a large serving bowl. Add the bell peppers, spinach, carrots, sun-dried tomatoes, basil, olives, and feta. (If not serving immediately, add the basil just before serving.) Toss together gently. Pour the dressing over the mixture and toss again, gently but thoroughly. Serve immediately, or cover and refrigerate for up to 8 hours.

Dan's Retro Macaroni Salad

No collection of pasta salads would be complete without a bow to the past, the humble origins of what we now think of as pasta salad. Years ago no picnic or church potluck supper was complete without the ubiquitous bowl of macaroni salad. If you like to browse through old cookbooks for the fun of it as I do, it's unlikely you'll find any recipes for pasta salads as we know them today; indeed, pasta was either macaroni or spaghetti, period. Italians have disclaimed pasta salads until recently, when some delicious recipes have been noted emanating from the mother country of pasta. Here's an updated version of the old favorite suggested to me by my good friend Dan Bryant, cook *extraordinaire*. Dan prefers to use freshly ground white pepper for this salad. He says letting the pasta sit overnight in the oil and vinegar is the key to the deep flavors, so plan to start this salad a day ahead.

- 1 pound elbows or pipette
- ¼ cup extra-virgin olive oil
- 2 tablespoons balsamic vinegar
- ½ cup minced red onion
- ½ red bell pepper, seeded, deribbed, and diced
- ½ green bell pepper, seeded, deribbed, and diced
- ½ yellow bell pepper, seeded, deribbed, and diced
- ½ cup diced celery
- ¼ cup finely chopped fresh curly parsley for garnish

DRESSING

- 2 teaspoons fresh lemon juice
- 1 large clove garlic, minced
- 1 cup mayonnaise, homemade *(page 19)* or high-quality purchased
- Salt and freshly ground white pepper

PREPARATION

Cook the pasta according to the directions on the package for al dente. Drain in a colander and rinse briefly under cold running water. Shake the colander gently to drain. Transfer the pasta to a serving bowl and add the olive oil and vinegar. Toss gently to coat, cover, and refrigerate overnight.

The next day, add the onion, bell peppers, and celery to the pasta.

To make the dressing, in a small bowl, whisk together the lemon juice, garlic, mayonnaise, and salt and pepper to taste. Pour the dressing over the pasta mixture and toss gently but thoroughly. Serve immediately, or cover and refrigerate for up to 8 hours.

Sprinkle the parsley garnish on just before serving.

:: index

:: table of equivalents

The exact equivalents in the following tables have been rounded for convenience.

LIQUID/DRY MEASURES

U.S.	METRIC	
¼ teaspoon	1.25	milliliters
½ teaspoon	2.5	milliliters
1 teaspoon	5	milliliters
1 tablespoon (3 teaspoons)	15	milliliters
1 fluid ounce (2 tablespoons)	30	milliliters
¼ cup	60	milliliters
⅓ cup	80	milliliters
½ cup	120	milliliters
1 cup	240	milliliters
1 pint (2 cups)	480	milliliters
1 quart (4 cups, 32 ounces)	960	milliliters
1 gallon (4 quarts)	3.84	liters
1 ounce (by weight)	28	grams
1 pound	454	grams
2.2 pounds	1	kilogram

LENGTH

U.S.	METRIC	
⅛ inch	3	millimeters
¼ inch	6	millimeters
½ inch	12	millimeters
1 inch	2.5	centimeters

OVEN TEMPERATURE

FAHRENHEIT	CELSIUS	GAS
250	120	½
275	140	1
300	150	2
325	160	3
350	180	4
375	190	5
400	200	6
425	220	7
450	230	8
475	240	9
500	260	10